MW00453972

For
THE HURT,
THE BLESSED,
and
THE DAMNED

Krista,
Thank you for "On Being" and the healing you bring.
Blessings and peace be upon you,
Brad +

BRADLEY SULLIVAN

For the Hurt, the Blessed, and the Damned

© 2022 Bradley Sullivan

https://bradleysullivan.blogspot.com/

All rights reserved. This book or any portion thereof may not be reproduced or used in any manner whatsoever without the express written permission of the publisher except for the use of brief quotations in a book review.

print ISBN: 978-1-66788-422-6

ebook ISBN: 978-1-66788-423-3

Acknowledgements

I would like to thank my wife, Kristin, and my children, Noah, Rhys, and Ellie, for their love, always.

For my parents: Ron and Betsy Sullivan

My brother and his family: Kevin, Darlene, Julian, Miranda, and Liam Sullivan

My mother-in-law and father-in-law: Roger and Sandy Barkerding

For those who helped in reading and editing: Kristin, Chava Gal-Or, Angela Holmes, Jax Hinson, Kim Milone, David Nelson, Lance Ousley, Betsy Sullivan, and Amy Waltz-Reasonover

For my mentors who got me started and helped me on this path: Jimmy Bartz, Annie Belford, John Bentley, Janie Kirt Morris, Lance Ousley, and Andy Parker

For my bishop, Andy Doyle

For the folks of Virginia Theological Seminary, and for Adam Goren

Use of Scripture

Unless otherwise noted, Scripture quotations are from the New Revised Standard Version Bible, copyright © 1989 National Council of the Churches of Christ in the United States of America. Used by permission. All rights reserved worldwide.

CONTENTS

Introduction   1

Part I Healing through Jesus   7

Chapter 1.   For the Hurt, the Blessed, and the Damned   9

Chapter 2.   Faith, Not Certainty   19

Chapter 3.   For God Alone My Soul in Silence Waits   26

Chapter 4.   Incarnational Atonement   34

Chapter 5.   AKA I'll See You in Hell   48

Chapter 6.   Lost in the Words   53

Chapter 7.   Storytelling & the Power of Myth   68

Chapter 8.   On Resurrection, Grace, and Love: A Way of Life   74

Chapter 9.   Healing the World from The Tribal God   89

Chapter 10.   LGBTQIA+ J   94

Chapter 11.   God as Trinity, God as Mother, and How This All Fits with a Credal Faith   107

Chapter 12.   Healing. Connection. Belonging. Love.   115

Part II Stories of Faiths Other than Christianity   121

Chapter 13.   Annie & Judaism   123

Chapter 14.   Inaya & Islam   130

Chapter 15.   Lukas & Atheism   133

Chapter 16.   Jax & Heathenry   139

Chapter 17.   Buddy & Taoism   147

Part III Sermons: Learning from Jesus' Life and Teachings   153

    Chapter 18.   Advent Sermons   155

    Chapter 19.   Christmas Sermon   168

    Chapter 20.   Lent Sermons   174

    Chapter 21.   Easter Sermon   189

    Chapter 22.   Sermons for the Season After Pentecost   195

    Bibliography   212

INTRODUCTION

"You must unlearn what you have learned."

—Yoda, *The Empire Strikes Back*

Recently, as of this writing, I met an engaged couple at a wedding reception (we'll call them James and Jaqueline), and in introducing ourselves, we talked about what we did for a living. When I mentioned my career as a priest, James's interest was piqued. He said that he practiced Buddhism, and was interested in my beliefs, wondering what led me to the priesthood. I thought for a second and told him there were primarily three things that led me to the priesthood.

- First, I loved the idea of Jesus, the idea that God became human so that we might be healed by being united to God in every aspect of our lives. I figured we already were, but with God becoming human, our unity with God was made more real for us.

- Second, having grown up in the Episcopal Church, I loved the prayers and practices of the faith that were intended to help focus our lives on loving God and loving people. The practices of our faith are meant to help heal us in the challenges and hurts of life. I'd found, however, that sometimes these practices became ends in and of themselves, blocking out love of God and love of one another, and I wanted to change that, so that the institution of the church didn't eclipse the life of love that it is meant to help us live.

- Third, I had grown up in a church which was primarily a "love God and love people" kind of church. It was not a "fire and brimstone," "believe in Jesus or go to Hell" kind of church. Nevertheless, something in the teachings about Jesus still led me to have this belief that "Christians go to heaven when they die, and all others don't." I didn't like this belief, and I hated the fear which this belief caused me and so many others. I wanted a faith based on love, not fear. Then after years of struggle, having found a faith based on love and not fear (a faith without the ridiculous thought that all non-Christians are "going to Hell"), I wanted to share and teach that faith as much as I could.

My purpose was to help heal people, as I had found faith in a loving God to be healing for me. My purpose was not and is not to try to make other people believe as I do. My faith does not require that other people share it. I hope to decrease the animosity that has developed between Christians and non-Christians over all of this believe-or-burn, fear-based nonsense.

Back to the story, the above reasons for my being a priest intrigued James, and he next asked me about challenges I have of tension with *striving to be good enough for God* (my words). I said I don't really feel that tension, although I used to. I'm not good enough, never gonna be, and not supposed to be. I'm a total screwup with lots of bad habits and issues I deal with. My focus in choosing not to do some things and choosing to do other things is not about shame or "being good." My reason in those choices is trying not to harm others, trying to be loving toward others, and trying to bring healing rather than hurt.

I still bring hurt and harm, so I also seek reconciliation, forgiveness, and making amends. That is the way of Jesus.

I then asked the couple about what they did, and Jacqueline said she was a Pilates instructor and that she loved her work, also because of the healing it brought to people. She found healing through spiritual aspects of our bodies, through holistic practices. After I indicated that I too believed in such things, she continued, and we found commonality in our beliefs—the nature of our lives, our needs for healing, and the very down-to-earth, in-this-world nature of that healing which our beliefs led us to.

For James' part, he said that with Buddhist practice, he believed in reincarnation and in some kind of judgment for our actions, i.e., if we're terrible to others, we may return in the next life in a rather unenviable state. I love that idea. There are consequences for our actions, but not eternal damnation for a lifetime's worth of actions. We are, after all, broken, flawed, yet beautiful humans.

James then asked me about my thoughts on Heaven and Hell.

I said I liked the ideas of both but didn't really hold onto either as doctrine. I view Hell as a place of needing to work some stuff out. I may not want to nor believe I need to. I may be pissed off, resentful, lashing out, and blaming everyone and everything but me for my problems, and causing all sorts of harm (deserved, in my mind). If so, how could I possibly go to / dwell in Heaven in that state? Maybe Hell is a place to help me work out what's going on in me? Maybe Hell is a place of my own making, the outward embodiment of all the darkness and anger that I have become? Maybe I can't accept the thought that folks I hate are in Heaven, and so I don't want to go there?

All of these ideas seem plausible to me, and all of these ideas fit with the God I find in scripture, a God who, when one looks at the whole narrative (and not just a few verses in isolation), is always striving for restoration, healing, and renewal. Even the punishments meted out in scripture have a restorative aspect. So, I don't view God as an angry guy with an eternal temper tantrum directed at the humans who piss him off. I view God as seeking restoration and healing for all humans, whom he loves.

So, there may be a Hell. It may be eternal, but it also may be empty by the end of time, as folks who are there come to realize and fully know the harm they've caused, turn from that, release their anger and hurt, and are then healed from it and from the brokenness within. Loved right out of Hell and welcomed into Heaven.

I view Heaven as wonderful, as life lived fully in love with God and people, with no limits to ourselves and the love we can share. Beyond that, I have only earthy ideas of joy and pleasure to give some approximation. For example, my loved ones with me; as many breakfast tacos as I want; Scotch all around with no negative effects; and the continued ability to write songs, strive for greater ability on the guitar, and to make and play music together with others.

That idea of Heaven and Hell makes sense to me. If, on the other hand, you have Hell as an eternal, angry God-tantrum place to forever torture people, you tend to end up with faith based on fear. Fear that I may "go to hell" for eternity. Fear that my loved ones might end up there. This fear can lead to so much hate, discrimination, marginalization, etc. If you fear Hell and you believe others are going, then you really don't want those others to be around you or your loved ones. Their presence may influence you and your loved ones, and that can threaten both your and their eternal salvation. Wanting those others to stay away, then, may be a loving response for those you love, but it is grounded first in fear.

That wasn't the way of Jesus. While there are places in scripture where Jesus talks about judgment and punishment, those teachings don't necessarily mean what has come to be the almost normative view of an eternal, angry God-tantrum place to forever torture people. Again, such a concept doesn't fit with Jesus' teachings or ways.

Even so, I needed to come up with a way of understanding all of this not by ignoring the scary bits of scripture, but by wrestling with them, taking them seriously, and seeing where they led in conversation with other parts of scripture which talk about God as love and Jesus as healing.

This book gives the ideas of that journey of faith that I took, of that wrestling and conversation.

I got to tell some of that to James and Jacqueline as well, and to hear their stories and beliefs. It was beautiful. As none of us had any desire to change the other, we got to share some deep ways through which we encountered the mystery of something more, something greater in this world than our senses could confirm.

For some, this "something greater" is God. For some it is a higher power or a higher plane of existence. For some it is the great whatever, and for some it is simply a mystery.

Whatever it is to you or isn't to you, I hope these pages may bring some healing in your life. I hope to share with you what James, Jacqueline, and I shared over dinner at our friend's wedding: "Spirituality . . . recognizing and celebrating that we are all inextricably connected to each other by a power greater than all of us, and that our connection to that power and to one another is grounded in love and belonging."[1]

Healing. Connection. Belonging. Love. That is what I hope to offer in these pages.

The Lord bless you and keep you,

Brad+

---

1   Brené Brown, *Rising Strong.*

PART I

HEALING THROUGH JESUS

CHAPTER 1

For the Hurt, the Blessed, and the Damned

Run to the exit, jump again into the fray,
Fighting every battle, every blessing on the way,
The warrior rides on today.

— "Fight or Flight"

So, rather than start at the beginning of my story—what I believed growing up, why I came to be terribly disenchanted with Christianity, and how I came to believe in Christianity as a religion of love rather than fear (we'll get to all that)—I figured I'd start at the end, with how and why I believe all that "believe in Jesus or go to Hell" stuff is a bunch of hooey (technical term).

By the time I was in college, I couldn't stomach any variation on "believe in Jesus or go to Hell." I hadn't been raised to believe in that, but I had grown up to believe in Heaven and Hell as places we go when we die. I had also grown up to believe that Jesus saves us from Hell. So, while I didn't believe in "believe in Jesus or go to Hell," I wondered if I could escape such systems/theologies and still be a Christian. Many people seemed to have done so, but I still had to wrestle with it, to wrestle with the text of scripture. I couldn't just ignore scripture and believe what I wanted to in spite of it.

So, I thought, *what is one of the big proof texts of the "Christians only go to Heaven, all others go to Hell" movement?* An obvious choice quickly emerged: John 14:6: "I am the way, and the truth, and the life. No one comes to the Father except through me."

First off, a bit of background for those unfamiliar with the Christian Bible. For most of Christianity, the Bible is split into two sections: The Hebrew Scriptures and the Christian Scriptures, commonly called the Old Testament and the New Testament. The Hebrew Scriptures are the Jewish Bible, the stories of creation, of God's covenants with Abraham and Moses, of the formation of the nation of Israel, of the prophets, etc. The Christian Scriptures are all about Jesus, with four Gospels (books about the life of Jesus), and twenty-three other books, mostly letters written to congregations by leaders in the early church. Of the four Gospels (Matthew, Mark, Luke, and John), John writes of Jesus in the most divine language. John clearly calls Jesus "God."

So, in John chapter 14 verse 6, Jesus is talking about the fact that he is going to die soon and go to the Father (God), and his disciples say they don't know the way to the place where Jesus is going. Jesus replies, "I am the way, and the truth, and the life. No one comes to the Father except through me."

From that sentence, many claim that only Christians (or folks who believe in Jesus) get to go to Heaven, and all others go to Hell. Add to that passages where Jesus talks about judgment and some passages of New Testament letters to the churches which are misunderstood, and you get whole systems which determine who is in and who is out. Well, as my dad used to say, "That dog just won't hunt." Such systems turn God into a monster.

So then, accepting that Jesus' first sentence is true, that Jesus is the way, and the truth, and the life (otherwise, why believe in Jesus at all?), how could I believe that the second sentence, "no one goes to the Father except though Jesus," was also true and not believe that all non-Christians were going to hell?

Let's take a look: "No one comes to the Father expect through me."

Through: It's a pretty innocuous word as prepositions go, and yet various Christian groups have packed an awful lot of specific meaning into that one little word.

- "No one comes to the Father except *by being baptized at an appropriate age, having given a full confession of faith and turned one's life over to* me."

- "No one comes to the Father except *by being among those fortunates whom God has arbitrarily and capriciously elected to give the gift of grace to have faith in* me."

- "No one comes to the Father except *by having a conversion experience at some point in life, a rebirth from above, leading to a new life of faith and purity in* me."

- "No one comes to the Father except *by dying unbaptized or unsaved at a young enough age that, though full of sin, they are still in some unexplained but palatable way alright with* me."

Note how specific various groups have to be with that little preposition, *through*, in order to make it apply to their rules of "salvation." What if "through" was slightly less well defined? What if we looked not at how salvation was exactly conferred upon people, but instead at what salvation actually is (see Chapter 3) and who this Jesus fella is, through whom we come to the Father?

John 1:1, 14a

"In the beginning was the Word, and the Word was with God, and the Word was God . . . and the Word became flesh and lived among us . . ."

Ok, so according to this, God is the Word, i.e., the Word of God which spoke creation into existence ("In the beginning" of the Bible, the first book,

Genesis). The Word became the human person, Jesus, and Jesus calls God "Father." So:

- The Father is God
- The Word, i.e., Jesus, is also God
    - I know, it is terribly confusing—we believe that God is three persons and yet one God. This idea is called "The Trinity," and there is a lengthier discourse on that in Chapter 11.

Now we get to read John 14:6 as follows:

- "I am the way, and the truth, and the life, no one comes to the Father except through the Word of God, which is God." I.e., the only way to God is through God. I.e., Jesus is claiming to be God.
- John 14:6 is less expressing a requirement for how one is to come to the Father as it is a statement expressing Jesus' identity.

Add to this . . .

Genesis 1:3

"Then God said, 'Let there be light'; and there was light."

God spoke creation into existence through God's Word. God's Word is eternal, and I believe, still present and active in creation.

And . . .

Genesis 15:1, Exodus 20:1, and Isaiah 39:5, etc.

"After these things the word of the Lord came to Abram in a vision, 'Do not be afraid, Abram, I am your shield; your reward shall be very great.'"

"Then God spoke all these words." (The 10 Commandments)

"Then Isaiah said to Hezekiah, 'Hear the word of the Lord of Hosts: The grass withers, the flower fades; but the word of our God will stand for ever.'"

The Word of God which spoke creation into existence, spoke to God's people and was spoken through the law of Israel and the prophets.

Also . . .

Romans 1:20

"Ever since the creation of the world, [God's] eternal power and divine nature, invisible though they are, have been understood and seen through the things which he has made."

God's Word, which spoke creation into existence, is still present and active in creation, and God can be seen and understood through nature, through all of creation.

Finally, we add Matthew 25:31–46 *(summed up below)*:

". . . Come, you that are blessed by my Father, inherit the kingdom prepared for you from the foundation of the world; for I was hungry and you gave me food, I was thirsty and you gave me something to drink, I was a stranger and you welcomed me, I was naked and you gave me clothing, I was sick and you took care of me, I was in prison and you visited me . . . Truly I tell you, just as you did it to one of the least of these who are members of my family, you did it to me . . ."

This passage is Jesus telling about the eventual judgment of the nations, i.e., the Gentiles, the folks who aren't Jewish, who don't necessarily believe in any kind of deity, and who certainly don't believe in Jesus or in the God of Israel. Jesus welcomes them into the Kingdom of his Father because they treated others with compassion, mercy, kindness, and love. They are still coming to the Father through Jesus.

From the above, we can conclude a few things:

- Coming to God through the law and the prophets is coming to God through the Word of God, i.e., Jesus.

- Coming to God through somehow recognizing God in nature or anything at all in creation is coming to God through the Word of God still present and active in creation, i.e., Jesus.

- Those who are merciful, compassionate, kind, and loving are welcomed into the Kingdom of the Father by the Son, still coming to the Father through the Word of God, i.e., Jesus.

Believing Jesus to be the Word of God which spoke creation into existence and which spoke through the law and the prophets, we believe Jesus to be much more than a historic man who lived in Israel a couple thousand years ago. We believe Jesus to be God and therefore to be in and through all of creation, while also being human and living a human life for thirty or so years. Coming to the Father *through* Jesus, therefore, can happen in a multitude of ways, some of which have nothing to do with belief in Jesus, or necessarily belief in anything at all.

In other words, the belief that Jesus is God does not limit who gets to be with God. A belief in Jesus does not necessitate a belief in the damnation of anyone. A belief in Jesus is, rather, a way to come to a connection to God and to live with love and belonging.

This brings us far from the fear-inspired darkness of certainty and rules (of who's in and who's out) and into the wonder-inspired beauty of love and mystery.

- *But wait! Doesn't the Matthew passage about Jesus welcoming people into his Kingdom because they were kind to others sound like earning one's salvation through good works, and isn't that a big problem for the "being saved through Jesus" idea?*

  - It sure does, and it sure is . . . if we're still into the whole question of determining who's in and who's out. If we still think the only point of Jesus was to determine what happens to us when we die, then yes, Matthew 25:31–46 basically tells us that at the end of time, Jesus says, "Thank you, come on in," to the kind people who were loving toward others, and "I don't really know you or need you around," to the folks who treated others terribly.

- For many, this is a problem because they feel it is "works righteousness," meaning that we earn our salvation and Jesus, therefore, died for nothing. Well, I say Jesus brings people to God in many more ways than narrow systems and theologies will allow. As for Jesus dying for nothing, that is a part of "substitutionary atonement," one particular system/theology which will be discussed in Chapter 4.

- *This doesn't sound like much of an airtight system.*
  - It isn't. It isn't airtight, nor is it a system.

- *Then how do I know that I'm saved?*
  - First of all, remember that salvation is not some calculus about where you go when you die. Second, trust in Jesus and in the goodness of God, and seek to follow Jesus' way.

- *So, salvation isn't just some way of determining whether or not an angry god-fiend thing makes you suffer eternally?*
  - No. Salvation is God's way, God's love, God's life woven in and through all of creation: through our lives and throughout our lives. There is a myriad of things from which people need to be saved: loneliness, depression, violence, addiction, fear, poor relationships, financial difficulties, illness, etc.
  - We hardly need to invent some eternal fire of everlasting torment and damnation in order to have something from which Jesus saves us.
  - That's just taking the good news of Jesus which is wonderful and mysterious, and turning it into something concrete and terrible.

The good news of Jesus is not:

- God made us, and we sinned, so now we're destined for eternal torture as punishment by this really vengeful, unforgiving, arbitrary, and capricious God . . . that is, unless we somehow have the right calculus applied to us to bring us to have faith in Jesus, be baptized in his name, or call upon him for salvation.

The good news of Jesus is:

- There is a God who made everything that is. God loves us, forgives, us, and cares deeply about us. God even shows us how to live so that we might honor, respect, and love one another. God then figures it'll be a good idea to become human, to share our lives with us and grant us nearness and understanding. Finally, God shows us that death is not the end of life, but a change from life to life. We needn't worry and fear, therefore, over all of the things about which we worry and fear.

As for Judgment . . .

. . . Yes, Jesus talks about judgment quite a few times. So, let's look at this idea of hell. Rather than a traditional scare tactic model of everlasting torture for people by an angry god-fiend demon thing, let's take a look at hell based on the idea of God as love, as eternally seeking healing, restoration, and reconciliation with all of creation. So . . .

Hell may not be eternal, or people may not be there eternally:

In Jesus' teachings about judgment, he talks of people not able to enter the kingdom of God and therefore needing to be cast into "Hell." It is actually "Gehenna," the valley outside of Jerusalem, which was a burning garbage pit (and a loathsome place where Israelites had once sacrificed children in fire to the demigod Molech). So, Jesus was possibly speaking metaphorically, using Gehenna as a symbol of divine judgment (or he was saying that living humans needed to be burned alive in the fire pit of Gehenna—which I don't see as likely). Assuming then that Gehenna was a metaphor for God's divine judgment, might there be some hyperbole in his teaching? Well, he wouldn't be the first to use such a device to drive home a point.

Looking then at some of the apocalyptic teachings of Jesus and at Revelation, the stories of such literature are not likely to be intended to be understood literally; rather they are giving image and voice to the presence and workings of God against the evils we do to one another and upon the earth. In the end, God is victorious, and no evil shall remain.

Does that mean that those whom God deems too much on the evil side (50.00001% evil?) will be destroyed in one way or another, and those who are only 49.999999% evil will be ok? Hard to know, and of course the numbers are both meaningless and illustrative. When we try to come up with some exact system to determine who is in and who is out, we end up making God's judgment rather ridiculous.

In 1 Peter 3:18–20, Peter claims that Jesus preached a message to those spirits in prison who had been disobedient in the time of Noah. In context, it seems that the message Jesus proclaimed was a message of salvation, indicating that those who had been in prison were able to be released and return with Jesus. So, after millennia in "prison," these spirits, the souls of the dead, were released. Ephesians 4:8–10 indicates a similar freeing of people from "hell", as does 1 Peter 4:6. Some have tried to make rules about this, that only those who died before Jesus' death were able to be released by him in the afterlife. That is certainly a possible reading, but also a very literal and narrow understanding of the scriptures.

Considering again that Jesus is God, the very Word of God which spoke creation into existence and which is present and active in all of creation, and considering that the same Word of God also became physically present in creation, I believe that wherever Jesus has been and in whatever Jesus has touched, Jesus remains. Therefore, if Jesus went to Hell, Gehenna, prison, the realm of the dead to set free those who have died, Jesus is still there (along with still being at the right hand of the Father, and everywhere else in all creation) to set free those who are there and desire no longer to be.

Considering also that in God's dealings with Israel there was always a redemptive purpose to his judgment, it seems reasonable to conclude that there would also be a redemptive purpose to a hell.

Assuming the possibility then that some go to a place of torment after they die, I also assume that the place of torment is not simply for the sake of retributive justice but also for restorative justice: that we will see and understand the harm we have done. I also believe that Jesus is there as well, constantly present, so when folks turn to him in remorse and ask for release, he is there to release them.

The above idea is also catalogued in some stories of near-death experiences. Rev. John Price, who was a priest in the Episcopal Diocese of Texas, collected hundreds of stories of near-death experiences. In those stories, some people who had died found themselves in a place of love and peace, while others found themselves in a place of torment. Those who experienced torment were those who were truly cruel. Some asked Jesus for help and release, and Jesus took them from the place of torment.[2] Then they came back to life (via CPR) and amended their ways.

So, by how I read scripture, by reason, and by stories of actual people, I have concluded that there very well may be a hell, that hell may be eternal, and that if hell is populated unto eternity, it is because people choose to stay.

I may be wrong, and I'm ok with that. I can never know if I am wrong or right in this life. What I can do is live a life of love and faith rather than a life of faith and fear. The "believe in Jesus or go to Hell" path led me to faith and fear. Leaving that path and following the path laid out above has led me to a way of love and faith. I'm still working on it, replacing fear with love, and I likely always will be, but this path continues to heal me, and I am hopeful and optimistic as I see where it continues to lead.

---

2   John Price, *Revealing Heaven The Christian Case for Near-Death Experiences* (HarperCollins, 2013).

CHAPTER 2

Faith, Not Certainty

"It's not about making sense. It's about believing in something and letting that belief be real enough to change your life. It's about faith. You don't fix faith . . . it fixes you."

— Shepherd Book, *Firefly*, Episode: "Jaynestown"

The quote above comes from one of my favorite TV shows, *Firefly*, created by Joss Whedon. I'm a sci-fi nerd, and I love Westerns, and *Firefly* combines both. Several hundred years in the future, the people of Earth have colonized many planets and moons in a new solar system, and in this future, our scrappy band of heroes lives on a transport ship called *Serenity*, captained by Malcom Reynolds. Mal and his crew transport cargo (not always legally), take on passengers, and try to avoid the Alliance, the rather less than good-natured interplanetary government that will destroy whole civilizations to maintain their idea of order.

In the episode quoted, two of the passengers on *Serenity* are left aboard while the others are doing a less than legal job. The two on board are a brilliant young girl, River, whom the Alliance has experimented on and traumatized, and a shepherd (Christian clergy type person) named Derrial

Book. Shepherd Book is looking after River, and he sees her writing in and tearing pages out of his Bible. She says she is fixing it, noting how many contradictions and false logistics there are. "It's broken; it doesn't make sense," River says. Shepherd Book then responds with the quote above: "It's not about making sense. It's about believing in something and letting that belief be real enough to change your life. It's about faith. You don't fix faith, River; it fixes you."

Faith—believing in something even though you don't know if it is true. Ok, that definition is rather obvious, but for years, around thirty of them, I was trying to make sense of my faith. I had this need to know whether or not it was true, like the way I know two plus two equals four is true. I wondered, I questioned, and I wrestled with faith, constantly trying to get to the point that it all made sense enough to me to become irrefutable.

I never got there.

I was pretty ok with the God idea. While I wasn't absolutely certain about God, the idea that something got this whole universe going seemed reasonable enough for me to run with it without too much trouble. Add to God creating everything the idea that "God is love," from 1 John 4:16, and I was increasingly secure in believing that there is a God who made everything and that this God is good and loving. I should say rather that I was secure in choosing to believe. My belief in God was and remains a choice.

So, I could choose to believe in God, but throw Jesus into the mix, and things became more difficult for me. A lot of the difficulty centered around the exclusionary nature of so much of Christianity. Could I believe in a God that would damn most people to an eternity of torture? Realizing I could not believe that (or accepting that if it was true, I'd gladly be in hell, far away from any God who would do that), I was able to believe instead in something like the Christianity I have written about thus far.

Even so, I wondered if anything about Jesus being God was true. Was he just a guy, a prophet, a miracle worker in whom God's Spirit was especially strong, but not actually God? Even worse, was he a charlatan whose misleading of so many people finally caught up with him?

For a time, I took solace in the fact that his disciples continued to believe in him and to proclaim his resurrection after he had been killed. They wouldn't have done that if it hadn't actually happened, would they? That kept me going for some years. Then, I began considering the shame they would have felt if Jesus was a charlatan or even if he believed in what he said but was just wrong. It began to seem possible that the disciples could have made up stories about his resurrection. Having given up much to follow him and having believed in him so strongly, the letdown and disillusionment could have been too great for some of them, and so they might have made up stories of resurrection in order not to have to face the reality of their being duped.

What if that was true? What if Jesus wasn't actually God? What if I believed in something that was wrong?

That's what really got to me. I have a mighty strong aversion to feeling foolish, so I really didn't want to be wrong about my faith. Ultimately, this all came down to fear. Fear of being wrong. Fear of feeling stupid. I didn't want to be a fool for believing in this guy, Jesus, if he wasn't actually the incarnation of God. So, how could I know? How could I convince myself of the truth of Jesus' divinity?

I read and reread the scriptures. I studied theology. I looked at other religions. I couldn't find proof anywhere. Eventually, not wanting to feel foolish, I pretty well convinced myself that Jesus was in fact not God. That made preaching rather difficult. Yeah, this was while I was already a priest, working in a congregation, preaching every other Sunday. I knew what I would believe if I did believe, and so I was able to preach and continue to serve as a priest and as a pastoral presence for the congregation, but at times, it felt a bit like role-playing. How long could I go on wearing a priest's clothes on the outside while on the inside, questioning if Jesus really was God?

Rather than try to convince myself about the divinity of Jesus and explore my faith further, I decided to explore other faiths to see if they had answers which I hadn't found in Christianity. Considering all the other faiths out there, I felt the greatest affinity for Judaism. After all, I'd grown up reading the Hebrew Scriptures (the Old Testament, as Christians call them) and had believed that God had become a Jewish carpenter.

So, I began meeting with a nearby rabbi, Annie Belford, from whom you will hear in the chapter on Judaism. Meeting with Rabbi Annie began a great friendship and a beautiful sharing of our two faiths. We found respect and beauty in each other's faiths, and at one point, she asked me to speak to a group of high schoolers at the temple about Christianity for their confirmation class. They had questions about the Christian faith, which I answered from the viewpoint of the Episcopal Church.

They also had questions about Christianity and Hell, wondering if I, like so many of the other Christians they knew, believed they were all going to Hell. Annie asked them at this point if any of them had been told by their Christian peers that they were going to Hell for being Jewish and not Christian. Every single hand went in the air. Annie already knew the answer to her question. I had guessed as much as well.

I told them I did not believe any of them were going to Hell. "How could I believe that?" I said. "You know the scriptures; you are God's chosen people. We Christians are the also-rans, and any blessing we have comes through you. People who say you are going to Hell are talking out of fear and doing exactly what Jesus told his followers not to do, which was to declare who was saved and who was not, and I think they misunderstand what salvation is entirely. You have a beautiful faith, with beautiful traditions and practices; don't ever let anyone tell you different."

It felt good to give such affirmation to a group of high schoolers and to help heal some of the hurt they had absorbed through their Christian classmates. My friendship with Annie continued, as did our discussions and learning about each other's faiths. At the same time, my doubts about my own faith continued to grow. Add to my doubts the challenge of being a part of a faith that has so many followers who would bully their non-Christian classmates with threats of Hell, and I really wasn't sure I could continue with the Christian faith.

With all of that on my heart, and with my friendship with Rabbi Annie, I was strongly considering converting to Judaism (and wondering what I was going to do for a living if I did). Then, as I continued to consider this change, I began to think more fully about giving up the belief that God had become human. That gave me pause.

My whole life, I had connected to God through this human person, Jesus. I had believed that Jesus was God, and what I didn't realize is that I had also come to love the idea that Jesus was God. I loved the idea that God had become human. I loved the incarnation, the nearness of it, the closeness of God being one with humanity. I loved the idea of God walking as a human being upon the earth, the soil, the grass, the flowers, all taking delight in their creator's touch.

The idea of God as one with humanity was so beloved of me that I found I did not want to give it up. I wanted the incarnation to be true. I loved the incarnation. I loved the idea that "For God alone my soul in silence waits; from him comes my salvation" (Psalm 62:1)[3] was made physically alive through Jesus. Loving the idea that God became human through Jesus took away my need to know. I could instead accept not knowing because my faith was no longer based in fear, but in love: love of the incarnation, of God becoming human as Jesus.

I realized the futility in trying to know with any degree of certainty. Even if I had lived with Jesus as one of his disciples, I would not have known. I may have been able to be convinced, but I would not know with certainty. Realizing that I could never and would never know with absolute certainty whether or not Jesus was God, the objective truth of the question became irrelevant. I loved the belief that Jesus was God, and so I chose to believe it.

---

3   "Book of Common Prayer" version of Psalm 62:1, *The Book of Common Prayer*, (New York: Seabury Press, 1979), 669.

Faith—believing in something and letting that belief be real enough to change your life. Through years of struggle, I had finally given up my fearful quest for certainty and had found the love of faith.

———————————

After this, I began changing how I talked about my faith, changing how I preached, and changing how I talked to parishioners in pastoral counseling. I more readily admitted my doubts which sometimes surprised people; other times, they said things like "Well, of course, you have doubts; everyone does."

Hearing people talk with certainty about their faith had always been problematic for me. People would say things like "I have no doubt in my mind," "I know absolutely," or "I heard God talking to me." I've always had doubts, and I've never heard God talking to me, at least not in a clear, unmistakable voice other than my own. I can say I've had inklings of God speaking to me or guiding me, nothing clear as a voice, but times when something would happen or someone would say something to me, and it felt like an answer to a question or a direction I'd been wrestling with in my life. Perhaps it was just happenstance, or perhaps it was God speaking through these situations, but that was left up to my choosing to believe that it was God working in the world.

It sounded like others had such clear, unmistakable communication from God, and I had inklings that I chose to believe were God. I had long wondered what was wrong with me that my faith was so uncertain. When I finally gave up my fearful quest for certainty and embraced the faith of love, I realized that nothing was wrong with me—it was faith after all, not certainty. Perhaps others had clearer communication from God than I did, or perhaps what others expressed as God clearly speaking to them were also inklings like mine. In either case, I appreciated the inklings that I got. They worked for me, and they still work for me.

Regarding people speaking with such certainty about their faith, I assume some actually have such certainty. For some, however, they speak with certainty while having just as much doubt as I do.

At one point in my ministry, I was a part of an interdenominational clergy group. We would meet weekly for a Bible study and talk about our faith. I was definitely the odd man out, being the only one who didn't believe that non-Christians were going to Hell. I was also the only one who talked about my faith without certainty, talking about my doubts, wondering if any of it was true, and choosing to believe out of love of the incarnation.

At one point, I talked about sharing these doubts with parishioners to help them with their own doubts, and there was silence in the room. I asked if I was the only one who had such doubts. Finally, one of the other pastors said, "Well, of course, I have doubts, but I would never admit that to the congregation." There was general agreement around the room.

I believe their hearts were in the right place, showing steadfast faith for their congregations in order to be good examples: by their faith, their parishioners could have greater confidence in believing. I'm guessing that works for some, maybe even a lot. For me, such approaches just made me feel there was something wrong with me for having doubts. There wasn't.

"I believe. Help my unbelief." This was the cry of a man to whom Jesus was speaking in Mark 9:24. That was enough for Jesus. He didn't lambast the man for his doubt. He accepted what faith the man had.

There is nothing wrong with our doubts. Of course we doubt. We're talking about faith, and the opposite of faith is not doubt. The opposite of faith is certainty. If we have certainty, then we really don't have faith, believing in something even though you don't know if it is true. If you choose to have faith, be ok with having doubt too. Wrestle and strive with your doubt, and be at peace with the uncertainty. That's where the beauty lies, even when it doesn't make sense. After all, "it's not about making sense. It's about believing in something and letting that belief be real enough to change your life."

CHAPTER 3

For God Alone
My Soul in Silence Waits

Cool mountain air, thin places up there lead me
back again to where I had forgotten or never known.
Let "what ifs" go, like so much melting snow.
It's summer now; the sun has come, transformed the winter winds.

— "Dreams of a Young Boy"

The title of this chapter comes from Psalm 62:1, "For God alone my soul in silence waits, from him comes my salvation." I don't know how many times I'd read this verse until one day, many years ago, this one little verse hit a chord deep within me and my faith began to make sense.

See, as I was growing up and began examining my faith, it began to make less and less sense. Is the Christian faith really about avoiding some place called "Hell"? How could that be? People are born with an eternal torture sentence placed upon them, but if they happen to believe the right thing, i.e., believe in Jesus, then they receive a "Get Out of Hell Free" card? That sounds more like faith in an almighty bogeyman than in a loving God.

I grew up in the Episcopal Church, St. Dunstan's in Houston, TX. This was not a fire and brimstone church at all. Even so, the undercurrent of "believe in Jesus or go to Hell" was still present in the world around me. I didn't know how I could believe anything else. We learned that Jesus was the savior, and we learned that salvation meant going to Heaven when we die. We learned that we were saved from Hell. So, that basic understanding of believe in Jesus or go to Hell seemed like the only conclusion of my faith, and as a kid, I didn't question that too much. I was afraid of Hell but felt pretty ok about things since I was a Christian.

Later on, in high school, however, I began to be less ok with this binary option. Could God really set up human life into such a system? At the time, I was largely going with "unknown" to my question of "could non-Christians not go to Hell?" God could do anything God wanted to, so that answer satisfied me for a time.

Later, in college, I started questioning more, becoming surer of the idea that our rules for salvation were not binding on God and that our whole system of there being two places you go when you die—one good and one bad—couldn't be what Christianity was all about. Then, in seminary (priest school), I learned about theology and where some of the systems of "salvation" came from. That just about broke me.

I couldn't believe in a faith that was ultimately about a "loving" God who had sentenced all humanity to an eternity of torture but who had allowed a few humans to avoid Hell by believing in just the right thing. Again, how could that possibly be true?

Breaking such a faith down a little further, let's say a person is born (as people tend to be), and let's say that person is born to non-Christian parents and never meets any Christians through their life, and then dies having never heard of Jesus at all and therefore has no faith in Jesus at all. According to the "believe in Jesus or go to Hell" model, that person is indeed going to Hell, no matter how wonderful that person is. In fact, if that person lives only a few minutes after being born and then dies, that person is still going to Hell, according to such models of Christianity.

That person's life would, therefore, have been utterly meaningless. The only purpose of that person's life would be to suffer eternally. Such a belief system makes God into a bit of a monster, doesn't it? Such a belief system also makes this life rather meaningless, or worse, something best to be avoided in the first place. Better never to have lived than to live only to be tortured forever.

Such a faith couldn't possibly be what Jesus was all about, and so Christianity couldn't possibly be about avoiding a place called "Hell" once we die. What then is Christianity actually about? What is faith in Jesus all about? Enter Psalm 62:1: "For God alone my soul in silence waits; from him comes my salvation."

According to that verse, the one thing missing in people's lives is connection and union with God. If that is the one thing that is missing, then salvation is bringing about that connection and union with God. Avoiding some place called Hell when we die, then, is not salvation; it's a scare tactic. Salvation is connection and union with God.

Throughout human history, humanity seems to be aware of God's presence and also aware of God's otherness. We long for Source,[4] for the creator of life, light, and love. In addition, we often feel a lack of peace within ourselves, and many throughout the ages have found that union with this Source, this God who is both present and other, is healing for our souls. God/Source has been revealed and understood in many forms for people throughout the ages, and yet in whatever form or understanding, people have found that times of communion with God/Source are healing for our lives, our bodies, and our souls. "For God alone my soul in silence waits" seems to ring true in humanity's lived experience. It rang true in my experience too.

When I read that verse the time when it struck a chord deep within me, believing in Jesus began to make sense. What was the point of Jesus? To help connect us to God, because that is what our souls are longing for,

---

4   God as "Source" comes to me from Rabbi Annie Belford; you can read more of that in the chapter on Judaism.

connection to God, to our creator, to Source. That very connection is salvation for us; it fulfills that deepest longing of our souls. So, to help us with that connection, God decided to become human in the person of Jesus. Our connection to God is our salvation, and God grants us that salvation by becoming one with us. "For God alone my soul in silence waits; from him comes my salvation." Finally, Christianity made sense to me in a way that did not involve "believe in Jesus or go to Hell" theologies. Finally, faith began to be about love, not fear, through connection to God/Source.

When I believed in God's choosing connection to us for our sake out of love for us, I had greater peace. God is for us, truly for us. We don't need to be afraid of some terrible punishment after this life. We get to seek and live the kingdom of God, the life of healing, connection, belonging, and love, here and now in this world and in this life. These realizations without the cloud of fear brought me peace, and they helped expand the ways I sought and experienced God.

I no longer felt that God's presence was relegated to religious settings or activities, and so I realized that experiences of connection with God could happen anytime, anywhere. I've experienced God's presence with friends, family, and other people, simply being together and connecting with one another. Music is a way I experience God's presence, sometimes in songs with both the words and music together, sometimes in instrumental music, the language of the music itself opening my heart to God's presence.

Often, I experience God's presence in nature. Every year since kindergarten, I've listened for the first winter breeze of the year. For some background, I live in Houston, TX, which is known for heat and humidity. For me, winter has always been a break from the heat, a time of refreshment and new life. I realize this goes completely against the ways of nature, that for much of creation, winter is the dead season, but for me, it was beautiful and magical. So, on a fall day in kindergarten, I heard a breeze going through the trees, and it had a certain crispness to it, the kind of cool crispness that comes from cold, winter air. Now, the temperature was still probably in the moist mid-80°s, but the sound of that breeze was in the crisp 40°s or 30°s. It was the promise of winter to come, the promise of life and beauty, of rest and reprieve.

Every year since that year, I have listened for and heard the first winter breeze of the season, and it has always brought that same feeling: life and beauty, rest and reprieve. It feels like a promise of fresh starts, a reminder of joy, a renewal of all that is true, and good, and lovely in the world. That first winter breeze is a reminder each year of God's goodness and presence in the world, of repentance and resurrection, of everlasting love.

Then there have been times when the world has suddenly changed and yet stayed the same, as if the veil had been lifted to reveal the majesty of God in and through all of creation. One such time was in Bluff, Utah, looking out under a clear blue sky across a desert plain to the red cliffs on the horizon. Suddenly, somehow, I was standing on holy ground, fully enveloped in God's presence, peering through God into all the world around me. Elizabeth Barrett Browning wrote of this experience in *Aurora Leigh*:

> Earth's crammed with heaven,
> And every common bush afire with God,
> But only he who sees takes off his shoes;
> The rest sit round and pluck blackberries.[5]

This brings to mind a Biblical image of God's presence in nature (when God appeared to Moses in a burning bush) and expands on that idea, that God can be seen everywhere and anywhere in nature. All around us is holy ground. All around us is the presence of God, and we can at any time and in any place be at one with God, for whom our souls in silence wait. One more experience of mine came as I was going for a walk outside our suburban home over a decade ago and I lay down beneath a tree in the front yard to stretch. Again, nothing changed and yet there was God's presence

---

5   Elizabeth Barrett Browning, *Aurora Leigh*, accessed May 16, 2022, *A Celebration of Women Writers*, 2022, https://digital.library.upenn.edu/women/barrett/aurora/aurora. html.

as everything had changed. The song I wrote about it captures it better than a mere description:

> Lying 'neath a pinewood forest staring at the night,
> The stars are shining with the moon, offering their light.
> An hour or two before the dawn, I realize I've never seen
> The world from this view, and it seems as though creation's new.
> There's quiet and there's stillness 'cept a gently blowing breeze.
> I close my eyes and listen as it dances through the trees.
> I feel them swaying gently as they rock the slumbering earth below,
> The life that's held within, at peace till life begins again.
> I open up my eyes and look once more upon the night.
> Contemplating life and all the years that have gone by,
> Some with strife, some beautiful, they seem somehow the same.
> The love and peace I see has somehow always been with me.
> And now the stars begin to dim. The night begins to pale.
> With it goes the glimpse of the world beyond the veil,
> But the vision lingers with me as the sun starts its ascent.
> As the forest slumbers on, I make my way back home.[6]

Then there is finding union with God through other people. For me, this has been times of seeing something of people's true humanity, their and my unvarnished selves, with no fig leaves hiding who we are. This has come in times of celebration and joy, as well as in times of deep sorrow. Something of seeing each other as true companions, even for those brief, shared moments, reveals the shared divine nature in all of us, and in those moments are glimpses of salvation. In those moments, we are revealed as a shared and common humanity, living our lives here on earth and at the same time, fully united to God and to one another in the heavenly places (Ephesians 1:20, 2:6).

---

6   *Before the Dawn*, Brad Sullivan

Then there are times of forgiveness, of releasing the pain of past wrongs and hurts. Such is God's nature, and when we live that release, we find salvation, unity with God.

I even find something of our shared, true humanity in the grocery store. We're all there for the same thing, a great equalizer: food. None can survive without it. Regardless of money or power, privilege or obstacles, we all have to eat. There, in the grocery store, we can see our common humanity very clearly, and in that is also salvation, a vision of our unified humanity in the divine.

Times of honesty and humility, of people being honest with each other, of taking down the shields, removing the armor and sword, and simply accepting one another for who they are. When we seek not to fix the other, but simply dwell together, accept each other, and love and recognize our frail beauty, we find salvation, unity with God and each other (Genesis 2:18, 23).

So, what about Hell, then, the opposite of salvation? There are of course many graphic images of fire, torture, and everlasting darkness which frighten people into believing in Jesus, but we don't exactly need any constructions of eternal torment for us to understand Hell or to feel some need for salvation. Depression and anxiety. Loneliness to the point of despair. Hopelessness. Desperation. Starvation. Betrayal. War. Hatred. Fear. Need. Lust. A hunger for anything just to feel ok, even for a moment. We understand Hell all too well, and we absolutely know of a need for salvation, salvation from the countless hells there are and can be right here in this life.

What I have found in Jesus is salvation in this life, freedom from the many hells in which we find ourselves.

What if resurrection and eternal life, then, weren't really meant as scare tactics to get people to believe in Jesus? What if Jesus' resurrection was meant to cast off fear, to show us that not even death is going to kill us for good, that not even death is going to destroy our connection to God and one another, that the longing of our souls for God is fulfilled even in and beyond death? What if we are already fully connected to God and one another in the heavenly places even now as we live our lives here on earth?

That means Christianity is not about scaring us into being good or believing in just the right way. Christianity is about removing fear from our lives so we can live well and be healed in this life. That is what I found in conversation with my friend, Rabbi Annie Belford, and I came to understand more fully that the point of Judaism (from which Christianity came) was not the afterlife. While there are a variety of beliefs about the afterlife in Judaism, life after death is not the focus. The focus is on this life, uniting with God and bringing healing to the world.

That is certainly consonant with Jesus' way and teaching. The Kingdom of Heaven which he describes is here and now in this world, the only world any of us actually know, and the Kingdom of Heaven also goes on into life after death. It forever has been and forever will be, life in unity with God.

This brings us to the second part of the Psalm, "from him comes my salvation." Our salvation, that union with God, comes from none other than God. "For God alone my soul in silence waits . . ."

CHAPTER 4

Incarnational Atonement

"I am one with the Force, and the Force is with me."

— Chirrut Îmwe, *Rogue One: A Star Wars Story*

" . . . from him comes my salvation."

The previously mentioned idea that Jesus died on the cross to appease a god who was angry at humanity is part of a concept called Substitutionary Atonement. This is a concept which I don't particularly believe, but the basic idea is this: God is mightily angry at humanity for the ways we turn our hearts away from God and from the ways we harm one another, i.e., our sins. We are stained, unclean, unworthy through our sins to be with God and to enter into God's kingdom (Heaven). We are all, therefore, justly damned to Hell, an eternity of torture. Furthermore, because we have sinned against God, against the infinite, no matter how much good we do in our lives, we can never do enough to balance the scales, to satisfy God's justice. Even if we were to give our lives as payment for our sins, it would not be enough. Again, we are finite, and God is infinite.

Jesus, therefore, sacrificed himself for all of our sins.[7] Being that Jesus was God, his sacrifice was sufficient, the infinite given for humanity's sins

---

7   * See note at the end of this chapter.

against the infinite. Being that Jesus was human, his sacrifice was proper, a human paying the penalty in substitution for all of humanity. Only a human should pay the penalty to appease God's justice, but only God could pay the penalty, so God became human to pay the penalty which only God could pay but which only a human should pay.

In so doing, God atoned for humanity's sins and made humanity right with God, Jesus, serving as a substitute for all of humanity. Substitutionary Atonement.

As a system, it works pretty well and even makes some sense. It also uses scripture, interpreting scripture in such a way as to give it credence. Substitutionary Atonement can be read into scripture.

There are problems, however, with the substitutionary model of atonement. One, the system binds God to our demands for justice. Why could God not simply forgive humanity? Doing so would not satisfy the demands of justice, says the system. My question for that is: "What kind of justice is God seeking?"

If God needs retributive justice, i.e., punishment, harm done to a perpetrator to equal the harm done to a victim, then Substitutionary Atonement works. If avoiding a place called Hell when we die is truly what salvation means, then Substitutionary Atonement works great . . . for those who, in one way or another, get to be a part of that atonement (and by the theories I've heard, that excludes most of humanity).

This is a second problem with Substitutionary Atonement. Jesus' sacrifice was sufficient for the sins of all of humanity, but only a small fraction of humanity actually gets to be saved through Jesus' sacrifice. Generally speaking, according to this theory, only those who (as outlined in Chapter 1) believe in Jesus in the right way are granted the benefit of the atonement. Most are still punished for their sins.

So, with Substitutionary Atonement, you have an angry yet loving God who needs to punish humanity for our sins, and then out of love decides to take that punishment on himself in Jesus, except that for those people who don't believe in Jesus in the right way, God's punishment and anger still get their full, unfettered brutalization.

Such a system makes God's love for humanity extremely limited. Such a system also makes salvation as union with God eclipsed by salvation as avoiding punishment. Fear, not love, is the prime human motivator in such a system, and anger, not love, is the prime divine motivator in such a system.

"For God alone my soul in silence waits; from him comes my salvation."

What if salvation is, again, not avoiding a place called Hell, but union with God in love? What if retribution was not what God was after with regard to humanity, but rather restoration, making whole what had been broken? We find both of these in scripture, but looking at the overall narrative, I find God far more interested in restoration than in retribution. I find God far more interested in healing than in punishment. Union with God in love is the goal, and through that love, union in love with humanity. Salvation is healing, connection, belonging, and love with God and with one another. Restorative justice and healing humanity is God's purpose in becoming human, in becoming Jesus. How then does God becoming human actually heal humanity?

Enter Incarnational Atonement

Continuing with the idea that there is a God who made all that is, that this God is love, creation, and beauty, we find within ourselves a yearning for God. We find some awareness of this creator god as something more, something beyond and yet right here with us. This feeling of and yearning for God, for the great whatever, is as old as humanity itself. Unity with God is the primary thing our souls seek, and not having unity with God is our souls' greatest sickness.

Further, we find that we are fulfilled in our innermost being when we are living in unity and love with one another. We find healing when we are restored with one another; when our barriers break down; and when we discover our common humanity, our common struggles, and our common joys, delights, and loves. Removing our fears and finding deep connection to one another, we find our hearts and our souls healed. We find that we are one—one with one another and one with God.

That is the idea behind Incarnational Atonement: Our souls desire unity with God and one another, and in the incarnation, God provides that unity.

So first, what does incarnation mean? Incarnation means to become flesh. Incarnation. Carne, as in meat, as in carne asada or chili con carne (I'm from Texas, so Tex-Mex is a big thing for me, especially tacos). Incarnation means for God to become meat, to become flesh, to become human. By becoming human, God joins Godself physically with humanity.

Now, even without becoming human, God has always been fully united with humanity. God created all that is, and all of creation is contained within Godself. As vast as the universe is, all of it is contained within God (or do we really think God is smaller than creation?). Being that we are all contained within God, we always are, always have been, and always will be one with God.

Being that God is also wholly other than creation, our union with God is often difficult for us to perceive. We are flesh, physical beings. Physical connection to things, people, and places is part of what we tend to need. Physical connection is how things are often made more real for us.

By becoming human, God's union with us can be more real for us. We are flesh and so God became flesh so we would more fully know, understand, and perceive our unity with God. God became flesh so that unity, connection, and communion with God would be made more real for us in our physical lives, in this physical world in which we live.

Enter Christmas, the birth of Jesus[8]

Every aspect of our lives has been lived by God as the human being Jesus. Now, Jesus didn't suddenly appear as a grown man and start teaching and

---

8   See the Gospel According to Luke for the full narrative of Jesus' birth.

healing people. He was born in ancient Israel to a young Jewish woman, Mary, and her husband, Joseph, sometime near the year 1 in the common era. He was conceived in Mary's womb, however, not by Joseph, but by God, the Holy Spirit.[9] He grew up in a small Jewish town called Nazareth, became a carpenter like Joseph—his earthly Father—was surprisingly wise and learned in scripture, and then around the year 30, when he was about thirty years old, began an itinerant ministry of teaching, preaching, and healing. His ministry ranged throughout Israel and into some of the surrounding gentile regions.

The incarnation began when Jesus was conceived in his mother Mary's womb—God became human. The incarnation continued with the birth of Jesus, with his growing up. The God that created the universe woke up every three hours crying for milk and then drank from his mother's breast. He pooped and peed as babies do and had to be cleaned up each time. He cooed, laughed, and spat up. He discovered his hands, learned to crawl and walk, went through puberty, got zits, and gradually became aware of who he was.

God who knows all and is limited by nothing lived as a human who was limited by a human's capacity for knowledge and understanding. Jesus didn't emerge from the womb able to talk, walk, and control the weather (Mark 4:35–41). He gradually learned and became aware, eventually even becoming aware of who he was, God in human flesh (John 8:58 . . . ok, most of John . . . ok, all of John).

This unity with humanity in every aspect of our lives is salvation. "For God alone my soul in silence waits." God unites Godself to our physical human lives, and in so doing, we find ourselves united to God in every aspect of our lives. "From him comes my salvation." Incarnation itself is salvation.

In uniting with humans in every aspect of our lives, there was still one aspect of our lives, which it seems would be rather difficult for God to unite to—namely, our sins. How would God unite Godself to humanity's sin?

---

9   Remember that Trinity stuff . . . see Chapter 11.

What is sin?

How about we call sin the ways that we hurt ourselves and one another, thereby separating ourselves from one another and from God? What is a sin? Well, if something causes harm to someone, it is probably a sin.

Now, let's take a closer look. Sin, as derived from the Hebrew word "hamartia," means "to miss the mark." Think of archery, firing an arrow at a target, trying for dead center, and instead you hit the outside of the target or miss the target entirely. That is what sin is like. Throughout our lives, we are striving for union with God, for union with love, belonging, and healing. As we strive for that union, we often miss the mark.

Our souls and bodies desire healing and soothing from whatever is causing us dis-ease. What our souls really want is union with God: healing, connection, belonging, and love. In our efforts to soothe our dis-ease, however, we often aim off the mark, taking actions that seem to soothe us at the time but which actually end up hurting us and others.

For example, it's been a long day, I'm tired, I've just cooked dinner, eaten quickly, then washed the dishes. I am making some tea so I can relax for a few minutes. Then the room gets louder and louder as one of the kids has the TV volume turned too high, the other two kids come in the room shouting about something they are arguing over, and I end up shouting for them all to be quiet. I lash out, hurting them through my shouting and hurting me through my shouting as well because I feel terrible afterwards.

Was I trying to hurt anyone? Of course not. My goal was rest. In striving for that rest, however, I missed the mark and took an action that was hurtful.

This is a small example, but even in big ways, people are usually trying to bring about some good thing, some soothing of the hurts within themselves or within society, some comfort from the fears which plague them, some rest from the burdens they carry. Then they miss the mark and harm people in small and big ways.

From the earliest times of our lives, we find fear and hurt creeping in. We find ourselves broken over and over throughout our lives, and we end up scared and scarred. We turn away from connection out of fear, and we cause greater harm out of our efforts for self-protection.[10]

Union with God and with others is our soul's greatest desire, and yet because of our brokenness and our scars, we turn from union and seek solace in other ways. Addictions run rampant in humanity, as do violence, anger, and seeking mastery over others. All of these things scripture would call "sin," i.e., missing the mark. Union, love, belonging, these are the things for which we are striving, and yet in our fear and brokenness, we miss the mark and seek solace and protection against harm. We miss the mark and harm others and ourselves as a result. That is sin. Through the ways that we miss the mark, we end up more isolated, more shamed, and more fearful. We end up harmed and separated, with less unity to God and others.

How, therefore, would God unite Godself to that separation? How would God unite Godself to harm, to isolation, shame, fear, and disunity? Should God live a human life in which God harms other people? Should God start wars, kill, maim, bully, and belittle in order to unite Godself physically to humanity's hurts and harms? Probably not the best idea.

Enter the Crucifixion, the death of Jesus

Jesus was killed as a prisoner of the Roman Empire, put to death by crucifixion in which he was nailed to a wooden cross and left to hang there for hours until he eventually suffocated. Rome executed many people in this way. How did Jesus go from a carpenter turned itinerant preacher and healer to a convicted criminal, sentenced to death?

Jesus' teaching challenged many of the religious authorities of the day in Israel. He developed a large following, and this was a problem for those who believed his teachings were heretical, going against the religion and the teachings of Israel. In addition, Israel was under Roman occupation.

---

10   For more on this idea, read Brené Brown, *Rising Strong*.

There had been limited Jewish uprisings which were viciously tamped out by Rome. Some of Jesus' followers then began to believe that he was a long-awaited messiah, one who would become king over Israel and destroy Israel's enemies, i.e., Rome.

Considering that Israel had a king already (albeit one who was a Roman puppet), and considering that an uprising would likely have resulted in terrible bloodshed for Israel, the religious authorities had ample reason to stop Jesus before, as they believed, he began an insurrection. Add to this their belief that Jesus was turning people away from God (He wasn't, actually), and it is little surprise that they had Jesus arrested and wanted him sentenced to death.

They implored the Roman governor to have Jesus sentenced to death; he complied, and Jesus was executed by crucifixion.

This is where Jesus has been called "a sacrifice for sin," understood as the atoning sacrifice to make God no longer angry at (all? some small portion of?) humanity according to substitutionary atonement. Incarnational atonement, however, has a different understanding as to how Jesus' death on the cross unites humanity to God.

Remember that with the incarnation, all aspects of humanity are united to God, and that unity with God is salvation. The crucifixion, then, is salvific because in the crucifixion, all of humanity's sin was united to God. Scripture describes this in many ways; among them: "[Jesus] bore our sins in his body on the cross . . ." (1 Peter 2:24) and "For our sake he made [Jesus] to be sin who knew no sin . . ." (2 Corinthians 5:21). In that moment on the cross, all of the sins of the world, forever and unto the end of time, were placed upon Jesus. In that moment on the cross, all the hatred, harm, and disunity of all of humanity were placed upon Jesus (who was also God, remember), and God took unto Godself all separation from God, so that nothing "in all creation, will be able to separate us from the love of God in Christ Jesus . . ." (Romans 8:39).

If ever we are separated from God or find ourselves in a state of disunity with God, God has already taken that disunity upon Godself, and so we find we are still united with God as ever we have been. That is incarnational atonement.

Then, after being united with all sin, all separation from God, Jesus died on the cross. In that death, Jesus united even human death with God. Nothing can separate us from God, not even death. So, when we die, we are still alive with God, our lives being "changed, not ended."[11]

Then, after Jesus died, after he united our sin and death to God, Jesus was raised from the dead. This revealed a couple of things to us. One, life really does continue on after death. When Jesus was raised, he was alive, and he was still human. He was changed in that he could no longer die; he could teleport from one place to another, and he could alter his appearance, but he was still human. He had flesh and bones and still ate meals with his friends (Luke 24:39–43).

The other thing Jesus' resurrection revealed to us is that even after death, we are still united to God. Jesus' continuing humanity after his resurrection reveals this to us. After his earthly life was finished, couldn't Jesus have been resurrected as some sort of "super transcendent no longer human being" thing? Of course, he could have, but that would have missed the point entirely. Jesus was raised as a human being because unity with humans was what God was going for (Ephesians 1:9–10).

When God became one with humanity, God was playing for keeps. When God became human, God was revealing to us that nothing about our humanity could separate us from God. Our lives, with all of our human imperfections and screwups cannot separate us from God. How could they? God made us with all of our imperfections and screwups, and God loves us.

---

11   Liturgy for Burial, Communion Preface, *The Book of Common Prayer*, (New York: Seabury Press, 1979), 328.

All of our sins cannot separate us from God. How could they? God desires unity with us and is even willing to unite with our separation from God to achieve it (or to reveal it to us).

Death cannot separate us from God. How could it? Even in death, our lives are becoming something new; our flesh is becoming something new. In death, we don't cease to exist. We are still a part of creation which is contained within God.

Life after death cannot separate us from God. How could it? God has taken human life after death unto Godself so that anywhere we are after death, we are one with God.

But what about Hell?

You didn't think I'd forget about that, did you? You'd think that would be the one place or state of being in which there is total and irrevocable separation from God. Some passages point to that (Luke 16:26). We're also told in 1 Peter 3:18–22 that after he was killed, Jesus went to free the spirits in prison. This is an admittedly short passage of scripture, and it doesn't get nearly as specific about Hell, torture, or the afterlife as many theories about such things do, but here's what I take from those verses. Jesus went to the place of the dead where dwell the spirits of those who have died and are at (seeming) disunity with God.

That is one more part of the incarnation, one more part of human life which God took upon Godself. Jesus even took upon himself separation from God in life after death. Now, remember that Jesus is the Word of God which spoke all of creation into existence, and wherever that Word of God goes, that Word of God remains. Jesus went to the place of the dead, the place of separation from God. Jesus is, therefore, still there. Jesus is in the place of separation from God, i.e., Hell, and Jesus is also sitting at the right hand of God in the heavenly places united to all humanity (Ephesians 1:20–23), and Jesus is also here on earth living in and through all humanity (Matthew 25:31–42).

What this means is that if ever one finds oneself in Hell, Jesus is there to release them when they are ready. Remember, nothing can separate us from God. Not sin. Not death. Not Hell itself. Nothing in all creation can separate us from God.

That is incarnational atonement.

---

* A further note on the substitutionary model of Jesus Dying for our Sins:

For a long time, in ancient societies, blood sacrifice was a preferred method of appeasing the gods. Animals were sacrificed, and in some cultures even people were sacrificed to various gods. What was needed to appease a god or to entreat a god's favor? Life. Blood. Blood is the vehicle for life, and so blood was what was thought to be required.

For the people of Israel, blood sacrifice was also used as a way to appease God. There was a major distinction for Israel, however, in that human sacrifice was absolutely forbidden. Animals were used for blood sacrifice—for cleansing the temple and the priests, as an offering for sins against the covenant, and other things (Leviticus 1, Leviticus 5, Numbers 18 . . .). These blood sacrifices were understood to be commanded by God as part of God's covenant with Israel.

In the Psalms and the Prophets, however, we often read that God was not really all that into animal sacrifice. Here are some examples:

*'With what shall I come before the Lord, and bow myself before
God on high?*
Shall I come before him with burnt-offerings, with calves a
year old?
Will the Lord be pleased with thousands of rams . . . Shall I
give my firstborn for my transgression, the fruit of my body for
the sin of my soul?'

He has told you, O mortal, what is good; and what does
the Lord require of you
but to do justice, and to love kindness, and to walk humbly
with your God?

—Micah 6:6–8

Hear, O my people, and I will speak, O Israel, I will testify
against you.
I am God, your God.
Not for your sacrifices do I rebuke you; your burnt-offerings are
continually before me. I will not accept a bull from your house,
or goats from your folds.
For every wild animal of the forest is mine, the cattle on a
thousand hills . . .
If I were hungry, I would not tell you, for the world and all that
is in it is mine.
Do I eat the flesh of bulls, or drink the blood of goats?
Offer to God a sacrifice of thanksgiving, and pay your vows to
the Most High.

—Psalm 50:7–14

God seems to be saying, "I don't actually want your blood sacrifices. What I really want is for you to treat each other well." Here's another example.

Day after day they seek me and delight to know my ways, as if they
were a nation that practiced righteousness and did not forsake
the ordinance of their God; they ask of me righteous judgements,
they delight to draw near to God.

'Why do we fast, but you do not see? Why humble ourselves, but
you do not notice?'

Look, you serve your own interest on your fast-day, and oppress
all your workers. Look, you fast only to quarrel and to fight and
to strike with a wicked fist.

Such fasting as you do today will not make your voice heard on high.

Is such the fast that I choose, a day to humble oneself? Is it to bow down the head like a bulrush, and to lie in sackcloth and ashes? Will you call this a fast, a day acceptable to the Lord?

Is not this the fast that I choose: to loose the bonds of injustice, to undo the thongs of the yoke, to let the oppressed go free, and to break every yoke?

Is it not to share your bread with the hungry, and bring the homeless poor into your house; when you see the naked, to cover them, and not to hide yourself from your own kin?

—Isaiah 58:2–7

So, how do we reconcile these two ideas? 1. God commands the people of Israel to give blood sacrifices to atone for sins, and 2. God also tells Israel that he doesn't want their blood sacrifices, that what he's really after is for them to live with justice, peace, love, and caring for those in need.

I have several ideas.

Perhaps God changed his mind? Perhaps initially God wanted blood sacrifice for people to atone for their sins, and then God realized that actually caring about one another was more important?

Perhaps God used blood sacrifice as an opportunity to teach people a better way? Perhaps God went along with blood sacrifice, since it was so in vogue back then, and he figured he'd get the people of Israel to kill animals, rather than people, and to turn their atoning sacrifices to God, rather than to a man-made idol?

Perhaps we were the ones who needed blood sacrifice, not God? Perhaps God was never that into the need for blood in order to forgive people? Perhaps people felt a need to appease God, to atone for their misdeeds, and God decided to go along with it for our sake. Could it be that

God decided to go along with animal blood sacrifice in order to meet us where we were and then gradually teach us a different way?

With the atoning sacrifice of Jesus, then, was God, once again, giving us what we needed? After centuries of God speaking through the prophets, telling Israel that he didn't want the blood sacrifices, that he just wanted them to live with justice and mercy, grace and love, the sacrifice of Jesus seems to me as though God was saying, "Ok, you still want and seem to need a sacrifice, so I'll be the sacrifice. Then, no more. I'll sacrifice myself by letting you kill me. I'll take all of humanity's sins upon myself in that sacrifice, and then that'll be the end of all this sacrifice nonsense. Humanity can rest assured that no further sacrifice is required, and I will have united myself to humanity even in their disunity with me."

In that case, the atoning sacrifice of Jesus was not because God was mightily angry with humanity and needed something to kill. Looking at the prophets, the atoning sacrifice of Jesus seems to be more that humanity continued to feel a need to make a sacrifice, and God chose to be that sacrifice for our sake.

For our sake, our benefit, our healing. That was the whole point of the incarnation, God becoming human for our sake, our benefit, our healing. The incarnation was God's act of love toward humanity, and the atoning sacrifice was one more way God gave that love to us, by once again being what we needed, becoming what we needed God to be for our healing, connection, unity, and love. That is incarnational atonement.

CHAPTER 5

AKA I'll See You in Hell

"I never take 'no' for an answer."
"How rapey of you."

– Jessica Jones, *Jessica Jones*,
Season 2, Episode 1: "AKA Start at the Beginning"[12]

While I was working on the first chapter of this book, a friend who was helping me edit this book called with a question about something she had just read. She believed in the ideas I had presented, and then she saw a passage of scripture which seemed to contradict these ideas, namely, Mark 16:16, in which Jesus says, "The one who believes and is baptized will be saved; but the one who does not believe will be condemned." "How," she asked, "can I reconcile that verse with the idea that non-Christians aren't damned to hell?" To be clear, she doesn't believe that non-Christians are damned, but she wondered what to do with that passage other than ignore it.

---

12 *Jessica Jones.* 2018. Season 2, Episode 1, "AKA Start at the Beginning." Directed by Anna Foerster. Aired March 8, 2018, on Netflix.

There were several answers which I touched on briefly:

- Did condemned mean to suffer an eternity of torture? Perhaps not?
- Was this a later addition to Mark (as is likely the case)? If so, did Jesus actually say this, or were his followers adding to his words to give weight to their movement?
- Considering that Jesus is the Word of God which spoke creation into existence, does it mean that folks who don't believe, i.e., folks who are against love, reconciliation, forgiveness, and peace, are condemned?
- Again, condemned to what?

These were all good questions to ask, but more important for me than the exact meaning I do believe about this passage is the meaning I don't believe about this passage. I don't believe this passage means that everyone who doesn't "believe in Jesus" is going to Hell. I don't know exactly what the passage means, but I do believe it does not mean that.

How could it? If Mark 16:16 and similar passages actually mean "believe in Jesus or go to Hell," then let's take a look at what that says about God.

The greatest two commandments God gives are "Love God, and love people."[13] "God is love," we are told in 1 John 4:16. That sounds pretty great. "Believe in Jesus, or go to Hell," however, means that God is ultimately telling all of humanity the following:

"I love you. I hope you love me back, but if you don't, I'm going to hurt you. I'm going to hurt you and torture you for eternity . . .

. . .Oh, you love me back? Well yea, that's great! Now we can be besties!"

Again, as my dad used to say, "That dog just won't hunt."

If "believe in Jesus, or go to Hell" is true, then God is telling humanity, "I love you, and if you don't love me back in just the right way, I am going

---

13   Mark 12:28–31 – paraphrased.

to torture you for eternity." That means that God's way for "salvation" is to threaten and coerce love out of fearful humans and then torture those who do not comply. That's what abusers do to their victims. "Believe in Jesus or go to Hell" is God coercing love and belief out of humanity. That's not love; that's abuse.

That can't possibly be true, then, if God is love. Therefore, I don't exactly know what Mark 16:16 means; I just know what it doesn't mean.

Let's go a little further and look at some of the damage of such coercive theologies. Back in college, I went on a mission trip with a college campus Christian group. Truth be told, I was going on the trip because I had a crush on a young woman who was going on the trip. We'd been friends, and the importance of faith to her had reignited my faith. Sure, I was initially re-interested in faith just because I liked her, but the faith became genuine soon enough. Spoiler alert, the relationship ended up as just friends, and good ones at that.

In any case, she was planning to go on this mission trip, so I signed up. On the second day of the trip, we were doing a variety of work: painting houses, leading a kids' Bible fun-time program, and going out among people's homes to talk with them about our faith. The goal was to convert folks to Christianity, and such a need to convert others was not a part of who I was. Nevertheless, I joined my group, looking forward to getting to talk with people about faith, sharing something about Jesus, and hopefully also hearing from them. It did not go well.

We were in an impoverished area, and as we walked among people's homes, we stopped at a woman's house, and one of the folks in our group began talking with her. They asked the woman about her life: she had very little income, struggled to get enough to eat, and lived in a very small, run-down house. Then, our group member asked the woman about her faith. She practiced voodoo, dabbled in a little bit of Christianity, and had a couple of other faith traditions . . . basically anything she could hold onto to help with the struggles of life.

Disturbed, but undaunted, our group member then asked, "If you were to die today, what possible reason would you give for Jesus to allow you into his Heaven?" Holy shit! I was done. Here was a woman struggling to get by, and we well-to-do college students were going to harass and bully her into believing in Jesus via some "believe in him or else" threat?

No. This was not evangelism. This was not sharing good news. This was coercion, abuse. Now, I don't blame the member of our group. That was the theology they had been given. The "believe in Jesus or go to Hell" theology they had been taught, told them that the most loving thing they could do was to try to "get this woman saved" in any way they could—threats, coercion, fear—anything at all to help this woman avoid an eternity of torture.

Unsurprisingly, the woman didn't pray any particular prayer to give her life over to Jesus. She didn't suddenly become terrified of whatever torment our God could concoct. I believe she had more pressing issues to deal with, like dinner that night and breakfast the next day.

Let's say for the sake of argument, however, that she had been terrified enough to have converted then and there to Christianity. What would have been the message and identity of the God she would have believed in? She would have believed in a God who had dealt her the hand of being in poverty, struggling for food and shelter, and then that same God was also going to torture her for the rest of eternity for not believing the right things. This torture-God was then offering her a "Get Out of Hell Free" card.

> "Believe in Jesus, and I won't torture you forever."
>
> - God
>
> P.S. I love you.

That's a rather monstrous God in which to believe, and a rather dim view of life to hold. This woman didn't ask to be here. Her parents had sex, and as a result, she was born. According to the coercive torture-God theologies, she was justly born with an eternal torture sentence, simply because her parents had had sex, which resulted in her birth.

There are theological reasonings for this woman's just condemnation (along with the just condemnation of all humanity), and we'll get to those in the next two chapters. For now, I'll simply say that if such theologies are true, then I'll see you in hell. If coercive torture-God is actually God, then I want to be as far away from that thing as possible, and if that means that I have to go to Hell, then so be it. Groovy cool, I'll see you there.

Fortunately, I don't believe in coercive torture-God, and you don't have to either, even if you are a Christian. As seen in the previous chapters, there are very different beliefs about God and salvation which you can hold, beliefs which lead to love, rather than fear.

So, where did such a dim view of God and humanity come from? How did the incarnation—God becoming human, grace, love, healing, and reconciliation—go from such a beautiful thing to threats, coercion, and torture?

CHAPTER 6

Lost in the Words

> *. . . but many birds had come along and eaten*
> *all of the breadcrumbs that Hansel had strewn along their way*
> *to guide them back by the light of the moon, and Hansel and Gretel could*
> *not find their way home.*
>
> — *Hansel and Gretel,* The Brothers Grimm (paraphrased)

Well, to go from grace, love, healing, and reconciliation to threats, coercion, and torture, you kinda have to go back to the beginning: the beginning of the Church and the beginning of the Bible. See, in the creation stories of Genesis (the first book of the Bible), there is the story of Adam and Eve and the Garden of Eden. In this story, the second story of creation, God made the man, Adam, and placed him in a garden in Eden. God told the man that he could eat of every tree in the garden except for the tree of the knowledge of good and evil.

Then God said that it was not good that the man was alone (notably the first thing in all of creation that was not good), and so God made a helper to be his partner. Taking a rib from Adam, God fashioned the woman, Eve. She was bone of his bone and flesh of his flesh, and they were together in the garden, naked and unashamed. They had no barriers between them, no shame, no fear, no hurt, no hiding.

Then the serpent, which was in the garden, tricked Eve, telling her that God had lied, that they actually could eat from the tree of the knowledge of good and evil, and that if they did, they would be like God. Eve then took the fruit and ate, as did Adam, who was listening to the serpent with her.

Immediately, they realized they were naked, and they were ashamed, so they hid from each other. Then they heard God walking in the garden, and they hid from him. As a consequence of their disobedience and of their knowing good and evil, they were expelled from the Garden of Eden. Additionally, the man would have to work hard to bring forth crops from the soil, and the woman would have great pain in childbirth.

The story is one which tells us why things are the way they are. It gives meaning to our lives on many levels. For example, the man and woman were made by God. They were made to be partners in life. We humans are made to be partners with each other, not alone but living in good relationship with each other. We are made to be "naked and unashamed." This isn't about clothes but about our relationships, not shamed or hidden but vulnerable, supportive, and loving toward one another.

Note how this story is also like children growing up. In an ideal parent–child relationship, we are cared for by our parents, knowing little of the world, certainly not knowing good and evil. Then as we grow, we become curious. We begin to assert our own will; we learn to say "no"; and we eventually learn shame, fear, hurt, and hiding. When we grow into adulthood, we leave our parents, leave the garden, and begin needing to work for a living.

While working for a living may not always be everyone's favorite thing in the world, note the gift of freedom that God has given us. Adam and Eve were free to obey God or to disobey God. That freedom is a gift. Our freedom has consequences, of course, such as the ability to do harm, but we also have the freedom to seek our own way, to love others, to leave if we want to leave, and to be welcomed back if we decide to return.

See how this story can convey meaning to our lives?

Early on in the life of the Church, however, many folks began reading this story literally.

The apostle Paul, who wrote letters to churches, letters which became much of the Christian scriptures, wrote of sin (missing the mark) coming into the world through Adam (the man). Then he wrote of grace and reconciliation coming through Jesus. Through the story of Adam, Paul was writing of the truth which we already knew, that we miss the mark in our quest for healing, connection, belonging, and love. Through Jesus, Paul was writing, we find those things for which we are longing.

The challenge came when people read Paul's writings and the Adam and Eve creation story literally. With a literal reading, folks began to believe that sin became a part of humanity because of Adam's disobedience to God. Then, through the act of sex (procreation), sin was passed on to each human, like a parasite, transmitted from mother to child. Add to this a literal and eternal belief in Jesus' teachings about God's judgment, and you begin to have the belief that people are born as sinners, destined for Hell, and only through Jesus are people not justly sent to Hell.

Christian theology began to be largely concerned with what happens to us when we die. People began to fear Hell and God's judgment. Leaders of the church became concerned with figuring all of this out. How exactly did Jesus confer upon people the "Get Out of Hell Free" card? Also, who exactly was Jesus? Was he a human? Was he God? A bit of both?

Fortunately, they came to understand and believe that Jesus was both fully human and fully God. Unfortunately, they also came up with rather specific beliefs about the certainty of Hell for all people through the "sin of Adam."

With that certainty then, they also needed some certainty of salvation from Hell through Jesus. At this point, a life of healing, connection, belonging, and love was pretty well eclipsed by a mighty strong desire to avoid Hell after we die.

Into all of this concern about Hell, a man named Pelagius (360–420 ce) believed it was possible for a human to live a sinless life. Jesus had done so, and given that we have free will, it was possible, however unlikely, that a human could keep making good choices throughout life. His ideas were controversial, and they did not sit well, particularly with Augustine of Hippo (354–430 ce), a bishop in the church of Rome.

Augustine wrote at some length about how terribly wrong Pelagius was. Augustine's basic idea was that if there was any way that a human could be sinless and therefore saved from Hell on his or her own, "then Christ died for nothing."[14] Here is how his argument went:

- From a literal reading of scripture, Augustine believed that all people were born into condemnation due to Adam and Eve's sin. All of humanity was, therefore, justly damned to an eternity of torture by God as punishment for our sin.

- In John 14:6, Jesus stated that "no one comes to the Father except through me." Using that and other passages of scripture, Augustine continued and codified a theology, that anyone who did not believe in Jesus / get baptized in the name of Jesus / call upon Jesus for salvation would remain justly damned. No one could avoid this eternity of torture apart from belief in Jesus.

- Now, belief in Jesus was a gift of grace from God. No one earned it. If they did, then they'd be earning their salvation. If they earned their salvation, then Jesus died in vain. Nice circular argument, huh?

- So, who got the "Get Out of Hell Free" cards?

  - Was it those who tended to be kinda like Jesus? No!

  - If their behavior was the reason they were given the gift of grace, then they would have been earning their own salvation.

  - Was it those who might be receptive to having faith? No!

---

14   * For a more detailed explanation, see the notes at the end of the chapter.

- If their receptivity to faith was the reason they were given the gift of grace, then they would have been earning their own salvation.

- Therefore, those who got the "Get Out of Hell Free" cards were random. It had nothing to do with their character or nature.

- So, what was the mechanism for determining who was predestined for salvation (i.e., who was in and who was out)? Election!

  - God elected from before all time who was going to receive the "Get Out of Hell Free" cards. This election was completely random.

    - If you happened to be part of the happy election team, then good for you.

    - If not, well, you were justly damned anyway, so God was still loving and good . . . as well as absolutely sovereign.

  - Neat, huh?

According to Augustine, even an infant who is born and dies .025 seconds after birth is justly damned to an eternity of suffering.[15] This infant in question did nothing at all in this world other than take a breath. For that, however, being not among God's elect, said infant gets tortured for eternity. You gotta give the guy credit; he saw his system through to a very dark place and stuck by it. Not even most "believe in Jesus or go to Hell" Christians have the stones for that nowadays; many grant an unexplained loophole for unbaptized babies and children (only those born to Christian parents?).

Augustine's system works perfectly and is airtight. Through Adam's sin, all humanity is justly damned to Hell. So, in God's great love, he determined that some would be elected to salvation and saved from the fires of eternal torture. God's sovereignty was defended, and, in so far as the system goes, so was God's goodness.

---

15   * See the notes at the end of this chapter.

There is, of course, a slight problem with the whole predestination/election system in that the entire existence of most of humanity is entirely without purpose other than to suffer eternally (and possibly to procreate and bring forth a descendant who may be among the elect).

Most of all humanity throughout all time, therefore, are nothing more than the victims of two people's sexual act resulting in procreation. Two people unknown to us at the time, have sex, and about nine months later, we are each born condemned, unless we happen to be among God's happy elect.

The system fits with some literal understandings of scripture and interpretations of the creation stories. The system also turns God into something of a monster.

Additionally, the Augustinian system produces a faith that is largely self-interested and fear based. There is love of God in such faith, to be sure, but fear of punishment is the underlying motivator in such a faith. Where do you go when you die? That's the question that is at the beginning and the end of such faith. Apart from not going to Hell, there is no real reason for believing in Jesus, following him, or living out his ways—not that you'd have any choice in the matter anyway.

If you happen to be among the elect, then you love God, and there is nothing you can do to keep yourself from eternal joy. If you happen not to be among the elect, then you don't love God, and nothing you can do will save you from the fires of eternal torture.

To be fair, St. Augustine and others were doing the best they could with the understandings they had. They were flawed, as are we all, and they are worthy of grace, compassion, and love, as are we all. I'm not a fan of Augustine's theology, and I have often been unfair in my estimation of him. In truth, I believe he was a faithful man whose systems of faith got lost in the words of scripture. Beginning with literalism and fear, Augustine and many others got so concerned with sin and the afterlife that they missed the point of salvation. In the effort to alleviate fear, the beauty of salvation as healing, connection, belonging, and love was lost in the words. Fear eclipsed love, and they missed the mark. Don't we all?

———————————

So, let's see if we can find our way out of the woods by looking at some of the tricky bits of scripture, some of the parts that could lead to a belief in this predestination/election system of salvation. After all, Augustine didn't invent the idea out of thin air.

Children of Wrath, Destined for Adoption

In Paul's letter to the Ephesians, he writes that "God destined us for adoption" (Ephesians 1:5), and that we all used to live "in the passions of our flesh," following base desires as "children of wrath, like everyone else" (Ephesians 2:3). You can see how, reading even just these two verses of scripture, one could begin to believe in an idea of predestination. "We were all by nature children of wrath," and "[God] destined us for adoption." Universalizing these two isolated verses, you could read them as saying that all of humanity is damned, and that a few people (those in the church) are destined to be saved from torture. God (pre?)destined that some small few of humanity would be delivered from their nature as children of wrath.

That is one reading of the passage, but it is by no means the only reading, nor is it an obvious reading of the passage . . . unless you already have that idea in your mind. So, let's look at those verses in a bit more context and with a less universal approach. We'll begin with an example from two of Paul's other letters: Romans and Galatians.

Some Context for Paul's Writing

Paul was an apostle (one sent by Jesus) to the Gentiles, the non-Jewish people. He preached and started churches among folks who were not Jewish. Remember that Paul was Jewish, as was Jesus and all of his first followers and apostles. The Church began as an offshoot of the Jewish religion.

Early on, the leaders of the Church wondered about whether or not non-Jewish folk (the Gentiles) needed to become Jewish first in order to be Christian. They soon agreed that even though the Church came out of Judaism, the Gentiles did not have to become Jewish. Unsurprisingly enough, however, that initial accord didn't fully settle the issue, and conflicts continued.

In Paul's letter to the churches in Galatia, we find this very issue playing out. Paul was writing to churches of Gentile Christians, churches which he had started. The issue in Paul's letter was that other Christian teachers/apostles (possibly sent by the apostle Peter) had come to the churches in Galatia and begun telling the folks there that they had to become Jewish if they wanted to be followers of Jesus. This did not sit well with Paul.

Paul's understanding of Jesus was that when God had become human, he had fully connected humanity to God and that nothing could separate us from the love of God in Jesus (Romans 8:38–39). If people had to become Jewish and obey the Laws of Judaism before becoming Christian, then there was something else which superseded Jesus. "How could that be?" Paul asked. Either Jesus was sufficient to fully connect us to God or he was not. For Paul, he absolutely was.

An Example of Incorrectly Reading and Universalizing Paul's Writings

So, in his letter to the Galatians, Paul wrote (paraphrased by me):

> All who rely on the works of the law are under a curse; for it is written, 'Cursed is everyone who does not observe and obey all the things written in the book of the law.' Scripture also says, 'The righteous people live by faith,' so obviously we are not made righteous by the works of the Law.

Paul went on to write (again, my paraphrase):

> The law is not about faith, but about following the religious actions of the Law. Since we can't keep all of those actions, and

are therefore under a curse, Christ saved us from the curse of the law by becoming a curse for us in his crucifixion—for it is written, 'Cursed is everyone who hangs on a tree.' So, in Christ Jesus, the blessing of the people of Israel has come to the Gentiles so that we might receive the promise of the Spirit through faith (Galatians 3:10–14 – very, very paraphrased).

This has been read by many as a condemnation of all of Israel, as though Paul is saying that any Jewish person who doesn't believe in Jesus is cursed. Many have therefore read this (and other portions of Galatians) believing that Paul is declaring the Jews to be cursed. Nothing could be further from the truth. The blessings and curses of the law were meant to give direction for the people of Israel into a life of blessing, not to be a "gotcha" addendum to their covenant with God.

Paul's Rhetorical Writing

Paul was a skilled rhetorician, and when he made an argument, he would tell you what the argument was, and then he would tell you how every possible way you might think to refute it was wrong. In writing about the curse of the law, Paul was using rhetorical arguments to support the main thesis of his letter.

That thesis was laid out in the opening verses of the letter: "Grace to you and peace from God our Father and the Lord Jesus Christ, who gave himself for our sins to set us free from the present evil age, according to the will of our God and Father, to whom be the glory for ever and ever. Amen" (Galatians 1:3–5).

What looks like a simple greeting, giving praise to God, is actually the thesis statement of the entire letter, and everything else in the letter is written in support of that opening. "The Lord Jesus Christ . . . gave himself for our sins to set us free from the present evil age . . ."

Paul was writing against the idea that the Christians in Galatia had to become Jewish, having already become Christian. They absolutely did not, Paul wrote. Either Jesus had set us free, or he hadn't. Since he had, the laws and religion of Israel were not required for those Gentile Christians. They had already been brought into unity with God. Paul went round after round with this argument, eventually telling the readers that if they wanted to bind themselves to the Law of Israel, that would be fine. They just needed to know what it entailed first. Basically, Paul was saying, "You have been united to God through Jesus, and now you want to saddle yourself with both the blessing and the curse of the law? Why?"

Looking at this as a rhetorical argument to a group of gentile churches he had founded, we find Paul not declaring Jews to be cursed, but rather making as strong a case as he could to this particular group of people that they didn't need to become Jewish in order to follow Jesus. How often do we also make arguments with people which, if taken out of context and generalized, could lead to conclusions far from what we intended? For Paul, his intention was to declare Jesus as sufficient to bring the Galatians into unity with God, not to declare the Jews cursed.

Further Clarification on Paul's Writing

We see clearly in his letter to the Christians in Rome that Paul does not believe the Jews to be cursed. The church in Rome was one which he did not start, and it was a church of both Jewish and Gentile Christians. This diverse group of followers of Jesus were seemingly united in Jesus, until around the middle of the first century, when Emperor Claudius expelled the Jews from Rome. Then the next emperor, Nero, allowed the Jews to return to Rome around the year 54. At this point, there were two distinct groups of Christians in Rome: the Gentile Christians and the Jewish Christians,[16] and each group seems to have been claiming superiority to the other.

In his letter to the Christians in Rome, Paul was writing to this divided church, stating that neither of them was superior to the other. To the Jewish Christians, he wrote, "You that boast in the law, do you dishonor God by

---

16   Kathy Grieb, *The Story of Romans: A Narrative Defense of God's Righteousnes.*

breaking the law?" (Romans 2:23). To the Gentile Christians, he wrote, "For what can be known about God is plain to them, because God has shown it to them. Ever since the creation of the world his eternal power and divine nature, invisible though they are, have been understood and seen through the things he has made. So they are without excuse . . ." (Romans 1:19–20).

The basic gist is this: Neither you Gentile Christians nor you Jewish Christians have any room to boast as being better than the other; your unity to God comes through Jesus, and neither of you is better than the other. Even so, Paul seems to be wondering throughout the letter if his Jewish brothers and sisters who do not follow Jesus are still united with God. Has Jesus annulled their unity with God? "Of course not," he concludes! "All Israel will be saved" (Romans 11:26).

Looking at Paul's letters in context and in conversation with each other, we see that any claims that he was anti-Jewish are false. So, too, with his letter to the Ephesians, we can see that he is not making a theology of (pre) destination, with salvation for a few and damnation for the vast majority. Rather, he is writing to a group of churches in a particular context.

Back to Children of Wrath, Destined for Adoption

Ephesians was again written to Gentile Christians, and in that context, we see Paul writing that those Christians of the churches in Ephesus were destined to be children of God through adoption in Jesus. In other words, their being made Children of God was God's doing, God's plan. They didn't bring it about. God did, and God did so through Jesus.

That is far from a system of Predestination/Election for all humanity throughout all time. He was writing to those churches that their unity with God had come through Jesus because God loved them and desired their unity. God desired their healing, connection, belonging, and love.

Regarding their being "children of wrath," Paul wrote, "all of us once lived among them in the passions of our flesh, following the desires of flesh and senses . . ."

We all, he wrote, followed the passions of our flesh—aka, if it feels good, do it. A life with a guiding principle of "if it feels good, do it" can become a life that tends to be rather selfish, seeking pleasure for oneself without concern to the harm that may be done to others. What does that cause? Disunity, harm, strife, wrath.

Paul is stating what we already know in our hearts to be true. Selfishness and living only for what feels good leads to a life of wrath (toward others and toward ourselves). When we live selfishly, we become children of wrath. When we live without thought or concern for others, we become children of wrath.

How do we find freedom from that life of wrath? Union with God through Jesus. Far from a universal proclamation of "believe in Jesus or go to Hell," Paul was reminding the churches in Ephesus that through Jesus, God had healed them from that life of wrath and disconnection. God had brought them connection, belonging, and love.

Predestination and Election? Not So Much

So you see, Predestination/Election can be read into various passages of scripture, but only when such beliefs are already held and then read into scripture do they seem obvious. Such beliefs, however, are not obvious from reading scripture in context, nor are such beliefs intended in scripture.

The story of scripture is a story of God creating humanity out of love. The story of scripture is a story of humanity being hurt by all of the challenges of life, as we well know. The story of scripture is then a story of God healing humanity through continually bringing us unity to God and each other. The story of scripture is not one of sin, anger, fear, and extremely limited grace and forgiveness. The story of scripture is one of healing, connection, belonging, and love for all.

So where does this leave us? It leaves us right where we were at the beginnings of this book with beliefs that differ greatly from the predestination / election/ "believe in Jesus or go to Hell" theologies. Augustine and others like him have been considered the fathers of our faith, and their beliefs have influenced the Christian faith for over a thousand years. We can honor them for their faith and faithfulness and even find beauty in many of their prayers and writings. That doesn't mean we have to agree with or adopt their theologies.

Look again at the beauty of the faith from an incarnational view. At the deepest levels of our being, we long for healing, connection, belonging, and love with God and with one another. God gives us that healing, that connection to him, that belonging and love through God's presence in all of creation, including in one another. God also became human to join with us in every aspect of our lives so that we could believe and understand that nothing in all of creation can separate us from God.

We can remember that God has redemptive purposes, even in God's judgments. We need not fear, therefore, anything in all creation. Our faith in God can be based on love, not fear.[17] We can have faith in God that is joyful, bringing healing, connection, belonging, and love. "For God alone my soul in silence waits; from him comes my salvation."

* Notes on Predestination/Election

1. **Augustine's idea of Christ dying for nothing**

   This was based on many verses of scripture. The quote "then Christ died for nothing," in particular, was taken from the Apostle Paul's letter to the churches in Galatia (chapter 2 verse 21) in which he was arguing that they didn't have to become Jewish first in order to be Christian. The full quote is: "I do not nullify the grace of God; for if justification comes through the law, then Christ died for nothing." In a long argument, Paul was saying that the Gentiles in Galatia

---

17   ** See note at the end of this chapter.

really didn't have to first conform to "the law" of Israel in order to be followers of Jesus.

Augustine, however, used this and other parts of scripture to lay out his case against Pelagius. If, as Augustine wrote, a person could live a sinless life, then there would have been no reason for Jesus to save people from Hell, and therefore Jesus died for nothing. Ultimately, Augustine was defending God's sovereignty, something which I don't believe needed his defense.

2. **Augustine's belief that unbaptized infants go to Hell**

In his writing "On Nature and Grace," chapter 9, Augustine wrote against Pelagius:

Chapter 9 [VIII.]—Even They Who Were Not Able to Be Justified Are Condemned

See what [Pelagius] has said. I, however, affirm that an infant born in a place where it was not possible for him to be admitted to the baptism of Christ, and being overtaken by death, was placed in such circumstances, that is to say, died without the bath of regeneration, because it was not possible for him to be otherwise. [Pelagius] would therefore absolve him, and, in spite of the Lord's sentence, open to him the kingdom of heaven. The apostle, however, does not absolve him, when he says: "Therefore, just as sin came into the world through one man, and death came through sin, and so death spread to all because all have sinned" (Romans 5:12). Rightly, therefore, by virtue of that condemnation which runs throughout the mass, is he not admitted into the kingdom of heaven, although he was not only not a Christian, but was unable to become one.

** Note on "The Fear of God"

We are told in Psalm 111:10 that "The fear of the Lord is the beginning of wisdom; all those who practice it have a good understanding. His praise endures for ever." The "fear of the Lord" here is not the abject terror of the Lord. The point is not for people to terrified of God. "Fear" in this case is more like the "awe" of God.

If "fear" means to be terrified of God, then it makes perfect sense that we should come up with a theology that leaves no room for doubt or uncertainty. The predestination/election system does just this. Afraid of God? No worries. You get to be declared among the elect, and you get to have certainty, rather than faith, so no more fear or anxiety. The system has a bow around it, and it leads to all of the terrible beliefs about God discussed above.

With fear meaning "awe" (and maybe a bit of fear), we get to hold God's mercy and God's judgment in conversation with one another. How does God's judgment work? Is it like the parable of the prodigal son (Luke 15:11–32), in which the son comes back to his father after a life of wickedness, and his father runs to greet him, overjoyed because his son is back? Instead, is God's judgment like the parable of the rich man and a poor man, Lazarus (Luke 6:19–31), in which the rich man has hugely more than enough and doesn't care in the slightest about the poor man, Lazarus, who is starving? After they die, the rich man is in torment and Lazarus is in the joy of God's presence.

Which one do we believe? Both. We hold them together. We keep some of the ambiguity. We take seriously God's mercy and God's judgment. Aren't we glad that there is judgment from God against the cruel and the unjust? Aren't we also glad that there is mercy from God for those times when we are cruel and unjust? Taking seriously both God's mercy and God's judgment, we get to live lives of love and faith.

CHAPTER 7

Storytelling & the Power of Myth

Thus the war began
'Tween Earth, and God, and Man.

And so for countless ages, the earth grew dark and cold.
She buried deep within herself the beauty held of old.

Until the day her children give up their enmity,
And live the peace which they once held in the land beyond the sea.

— "Fire and Water"

I've already addressed the idea of believing in something that doesn't exactly make sense. "It's not about making sense. It's about believing in something and letting that belief be real enough to change your life." In the last chapter, we also looked at different ways of reading stories of Scripture. A literal reading can give us some conclusions, while a mythical reading can give us different meanings entirely.

I say mythical rather than metaphorical because a metaphorical reading feels too limiting. If a story is a metaphor, then it has a particular meaning. The story is a metaphor for a particular thing. These elements mean these things. A mythical reading, on the other hand, can be more expansive.

The story can give meaning in many ways and reveal truths about our lives beyond what some metaphors can capture.

As discussed in the previous chapter, the Genesis creation stories can have multiple meanings for our lives. They can be read as myth in the truest sense of the word, stories which may or may not be historically accurate, but which nonetheless are true. The Garden of Eden story, for example, may not be historically accurate. If we were to invent a time machine and go back 6,500 years (or however far back we need to go), we may never find a time or place where a man named Adam and a woman named Eve shared life together in a garden named Eden. That story as written may well never have happened. An inability to place that story within the timeline of human history, however, does not diminish the truth(s) of the story.

As myth, the creation story/stories teach us much about God, about the world, about us, and about our place in the world. God made all that is. The world was made with order; with purpose; and in a particular way, with some things coming before other things. God created humanity in God's image, an image of love, creativity, and relationship. God created humanity to be in loving, honoring relationship with one another, with the earth, and with all of nature and creatures on the earth. God gave us freedom, and God gave us great knowledge and power, hopefully to use for the good and benefit of creation and one another.

All of these are lessons found in the stories of creation, and all of these stories ring true to what we find in our world. We have great knowledge and power, which we are free to use for good or for ill. We seem most fulfilled when in good relationships with one another, honoring and loving one another. The world is far older than we are and came to be by something, some power, far greater than we.

Now, those are lessons which come from the Biblical stories of creation. Looking at another story of creation, we have the Big Bang Theory. This theory is not based on myth or stories of faith but upon observations of the known universe and conclusions based upon those observations.

According to the Big Bang Theory, the earth is far older than 6,500 years, closer to around 4.5 billion years old. The whole universe is even older, around 13.8 billion years old.

The theory is that at the beginning of the universe, everything that now exists was compacted tightly in an infinitely dense and infinitely small ball of energy. Then, around 13.8 billion years ago, that energy exploded outward, becoming all of the matter and energy that formed all stars, planets, air, water, plants, animals, and people. Everything expanded outward from that one point and is still expanding. Then, sometime around 9.3 billion years afterward, the earth began to form around a star we call the sun.

Eventually on the earth, life began to form, first as single-celled organisms, and over billions of years, as the huge variety of plant and animal life we have today. This is part of the theory of evolution, that life on earth started as single cells which changed over time through mutations during replication, with some mutations leading to new species, better adapted to life on earth. According to this theory, humans evolved from primates and many other animals before them over hundreds of millions of years, the slow process of mutation during DNA replication in zygotes leading to changes in one species after another, which eventually mutated into the first humans.

The Big Bang Theory and the Theory of Evolution are vastly different from the creation stories of the Bible. Many find these stories to be in irreconcilable conflict with each other. I do not.

I believe in the creation stories found in Genesis. I also believe in the Big Bang Theory and in the Theory of Evolution. All of these stories give important truths to our lives and understandings of the world around us. The creation stories may not be historically accurate, but as stated above, they teach us truths about God, creation, and ourselves. The fact that the theories of the Big Bang and Evolution give different mechanisms for our origins than the creation stories of scripture doesn't disprove the existence of God or the truths of those stories.

Believing God to have created all that is, I can believe that God was what made the Big Bang go, well, bang. Believing God created humankind in God's image, I can believe that evolution was the mechanism by which God made humanity. Looking at the creation stories as myth, rather than as literal, historical fact, I can believe in those stories as well as in the theories of the Big Bang and Evolution without any conflict, seeing both majesty and mystery in the theories and beauty and truth in the creation stories. That is the power of myth.

For other examples of the power of myth and the power of storytelling, let's look at some of Jesus' parables/teachings. There are the two parables mentioned in the previous chapter, the prodigal son (Luke 15:11–32) and the rich man and Lazarus (Luke 6:19–31), which give us some understandings of God's mercy and judgment.

Another parable is that of the laborers in the vineyard (Matthew 20:1–16). In this parable of the Kingdom of God, a man owns a vineyard and hires people to work in his vineyard. Early in the morning, he hires workers, offering them the usual daily wage. Throughout the day, he hires more workers, each beginning later and later in the day. When the time comes to settle up with the workers, the owner of the vineyard pays all of them equally, giving even those who only worked an hour a full day's wage.

What are we to make of this story? What does it tell us about the Kingdom of God, and what exactly is the Kingdom of God that the story describes?

One common interpretation is that the story is about God's extravagant generosity in letting people go to heaven when they die. According to this interpretation, the Kingdom of God is Heaven, which people get to go to after they die. Those who lived a good life / believed in Jesus throughout their lives get to be in Heaven just as much as those who only began believing in Jesus / living good lives at the very end of their lives. Ok, not bad, and that shows something of God's mercy and God's love toward all people, not only those whom society deems worthy. Add to that the idea that many of those workers who only worked for an hour are folks who never believed in Jesus at all, and I'll say that's a pretty decent interpretation.

Another, very different interpretation is that Jesus' parable is about the Kingdom of God here and now and the actual economics of God's Kingdom on Earth. God's kingdom is lived in and among us, present wherever and whenever we live out the ways of God's kingdom. By this interpretation, people need at least enough to get by in life, enough for food, shelter, etc. Also, by this interpretation of life in God's kingdom, people's well-being is valued above our concepts of fairness.

In the parable, those who worked all day get the usual daily wage, enough to get by for the day. If the landowner were to do what was fair, he would have only given one-eighth of a daily wage to those who worked only an hour. That seems fair, but those people didn't only exist for one-eighth of the day. They were alive for the whole day, and one-eighth wage was not enough to live on. Ultimately, if they were to receive only one-eighth wage day after day, they would die. Those who are shouting for fairness in response to this parable, then, are ultimately (and probably unthinkingly) calling for the deaths of those who only worked for one hour. That's not life in God's kingdom.

According to Jesus' parable, in God's kingdom, people have enough, even if it isn't what we might call fair. In God's kingdom, people matter more than our bruised egos. People matter more than our perceptions of fairness. People matter more than our fears of not enough.

So, the story of the laborers in the vineyard is a story with at least two very different interpretations. Which one is true? How about both of them?

The beauty of story and myth is how truths can be found in them in many different ways. Both story and myth reach deeply into the physical realities of life and into how we understand our existence to be. They also go far beyond the physical aspects of life, into the spiritual realm.

Story and myth touch on things unseen, things unknown, things about which there are only hints and allegations. Story and myth can take these unknown spiritual truths and make them real enough to change our lives. That is the power of storytelling and myth. That is the power of the stories and myths we find in scripture. They tell truths of creation and existence and even of life beyond creation. They point to the deep truths of spirit, of God, and of our lives in God.

CHAPTER 8

On Resurrection, Grace, and Love:
A Way of Life

Open wide the gates of hell and to the flames finally yield,
Face the pain that fuels the fire and lay down sword and shield.
Stop fighting all your fiends in your foolish pride and just
Dance with the demons deep down inside,
Dance with the demons inside.

— "Dance with the Demons"

One of the primary stories of our life in God is the story of new life and resurrection. This story is told most poignantly in the resurrection of Jesus, the new life of his resurrection showing us what is awaiting all people after we die. Jesus' resurrection shows us that death is not the end but a transformation into new life. In Jesus' resurrection, he also shows that resurrection is part of our lives here on Earth, and that grace, forgiveness, and love are part and parcel of the new resurrection life.

Shortly before Jesus was killed, the leader of his disciples, Peter, was asked if he knew Jesus. Afraid for his life, Peter denied knowing Jesus three times. Peter was racked with guilt over his denial of Jesus, abandoning him at his most desperate hour. That represented a death within Peter, a self-imposed death of him as Jesus' disciple. Then, after Jesus' resurrection, he met Peter on the beach, and over some roasted fish, he asked Peter three times if he loved him. Peter of course answered, "Yes," and Jesus responded, "Feed my sheep." Jesus gave Peter three opportunities to make amends for his denial and after each time, he assured Peter that he was still beloved of Jesus, still his disciple, and still entrusted to lead his church, to "feed his sheep." In his new, resurrection life, Jesus gave Peter grace, forgiveness, and love. That grace, forgiveness, and love then gave Peter new life after the death he experienced within himself, when he denied knowing Jesus.

Grace, forgiveness, and love bring about new life, resurrection, in our lives here on Earth. That's the idea of Christianity. We have many kinds of deaths throughout our lives: the death of dreams, of relationships, of times and chapters in our lives, of parts of ourselves, of identities we hold, and of the people who help make us who we are. We know and understand all of these and other kinds of deaths that we live with. Resurrection is new life after all of these deaths. The ways of grace, forgiveness, and love lead to this new life and are how we live this new life, over and over again.

In Paul's letter to the Ephesians, chapter 2 verses 1–10 (see end of the chapter), he writes about being dead through trespasses. Think about this as being alive, but also dead on the inside. Spinning one's wheels; treading water, too scared or stuck to move forward; addicted and living only for feeling better via the substance of addiction; full of anger and resentment, unable to enjoy the beauty in life. We understand these kinds of deaths all too well. We die these deaths all the time. Grace, forgiveness, and love, then, are the ways of Jesus which bring us from these many deaths into new life.

As an example of this kind of death to new life, there is a friend of mine whom I have known and loved for years, who was full of hurt and solace seeking, and for him, a common solution to his solace seeking was alcohol. He has allowed me to share his story.

He was (and still is) a successful, educated man with a wife and family. On paper, everything looked great. At the same time, he suffered from depression, anxiety, and his own inner demons. He was often sad, depressed, angry, resentful, overwhelmed, and on and on, and so he'd have a drink to take the edge off. Initially there wasn't much of a problem with his drinking. Over the months and years, however, one or two drinks would lead to three and four drinks, to five and six drinks. Occasionally drinking would become a nightly affair. Regardless of how much or how little he drank, however, he wanted that feeling of pleasure and numbing to continue. Eventually, he didn't want much to do with anyone else, including his family; he just wanted to feel ok, and the only times that seemed to happen were when he was drinking. He resented his family because they added to his stress, and they got in the way of him feeling better through drinking. At the same time, he also loved his family.

Realizing this was a problem, he tried cutting back his drinking many times but always ended up drinking more and never really facing the reasons why he drank. He was stuck, not moving forward, just staying as he was in whatever fears, resentments, and frustrations were gnawing at him. Dwelling on the past and trying to improve it, he was dead, motionless, existing only one day to the next. Things seemed fine from the outside with a good job and family, but on the inside, he was lifeless.

So, he had to stop drinking entirely.[18] This was something he could not do alone, so he sought the help of AA. Working the steps of the program with a sponsor, he began actually facing the challenges and feelings which he had been drowning in alcohol. Gradually, he began coming back to life and enjoying life again. There are still challenges in his life, but he's (re-) learning how to face them and move forward. He's becoming alive again.

That's the change Paul writes about in Ephesians: being dead and coming to new life. The man above didn't do so all on his own. He needed to rely on God, daily seeking strength and power to overcome what had become an addiction to alcohol. He also needed to rely on help from others

---

18   I am in no way opposed to drinking, nor do I think alcohol is bad. I am simply relaying this story as an example. Drinking is not "a sin"; it simply became one for this person.

in relearning how to handle the challenges of life. Resurrection. Death to new life.

This new life, Paul writes, is one in which we are alive in the heavenly places with Christ Jesus . . . right now, while we are here, living our mortal lives on Earth. The new resurrection life, being fully alive with God (which happens completely after our physical deaths) is already happening in our lives here and now, even though we don't fully realize or experience it yet. This means that life on Earth is also life in the heavenly places.

How's that work exactly?

Well, God is everywhere, in and through all creation. If we are one place with God, and God is all places, then we are also in those other places with God. Beyond that, I don't know exactly how life on Earth is also life in the heavenly places, and I don't need to. I believe it, and I let that belief be real enough to change my life.

Looking further into the "life in the heavenly places" idea, Paul writes that "in the ages to come," God will show the riches of his grace in kindness toward us. In the ages to come. In the future. There is something of a "not yet" component to being fully alive with God, in addition to the "already" component of being alive with God.

When might "not yet" become fully "now"? When might God show us the immeasurable riches of his grace in kindness toward us? In the ages to come. The ages to come could be at the end of all time, or at any point in the future for any of us. Five years from now? Ten? Maybe next month or next Tuesday?

Paul goes on to write that this new life is not our own doing, but it is the gift of God. Of course, it is from God. "For God alone my soul in silence waits; from him comes my salvation." God brings us to God, offers us grace, forgiveness, and love, kindness, and a new life.

So, do we have any part in bringing about this new life, or do we simply sit passively by, waiting for God to do his thing? Of course we have a part to play. This new life is "not the result of works," Paul writes, "so that no one may boast," but while we acknowledge that God's power working within us has brought about this new life, we still work to bring about this new life. There are also new works in this new life. The grace, forgiveness, and love which we embody help bring about new life. Those works are part of the new life, and we are part of those works . . . just as a life which leads to a variety of deaths is brought about through our works, i.e., through how we live.

As I wrote earlier, Paul writes about us (the Ephesians) being dead because of how we lived. Paul calls this being "children of wrath" (Ephesians 2:1,3). Being dead, though alive, and living as children of wrath is no big mystery for us, as seen in the examples above. Again, being dead through trespasses is living selfishly, living with an "if it feels good, do it," mindset, regardless of the harm caused to others. Being dead through trespasses is living with our shields up to protect us from harm so much so that we end up causing harm to ourselves and to others.

Such a way of life does not come from us being horribly and utterly wretched, awful people. Such a way of life comes from us being broken and hurting, seeking solace and protection in any way we can. God knows this.

We seek things that soothe our pain. They feel good, and we feel better, more alive, like we fit in (or like we just aren't bothered as much anymore). Such soothing remedies may be harmful to us in the long run (and even in the short run), but we don't or won't see it because we're in pain, and these things seem to help. We spin our wheels, seeking solace, even appearing on the outside like life is going well, but on the inside, we're dying, unable to truly live, to truly have the healing, connection, belonging, and love which our bodies and souls need.

In such a state, we feel and cause wrath. Saying we were dead through our way of life and that we were children of wrath is not a condemnation, therefore, nor is it an assurance or threat of punishment. Saying we were dead through our way of life is a description of being dead though alive. Being children of wrath is something that is quite familiar to us. The ways of life as children of wrath are things we do all the time.

We act/react out of our anger, unable to think clearly because lizard brain has taken over. Lizard brain is what I call it when our "fight or flight" impulse takes over; the thinking part of our brain is largely shut down, and the lower, survival part of our brain is doing the "thinking" for us. With lizard brain in operation, we're seeing red, and our angry actions seem perfectly acceptable . . . until later when we're calm again and feeling conflicted or terrible about what we did.

We are hurt, we develop resentments, and our actions are darkened by those grudges. We stop seeing the humanity of others and see only the ways they have harmed us. We see only the ways we feel they are wrong.

Then we often numb out, so overcome by life, that we spend much of our free time checking out of life, numbing the hard emotions. Of course, when we do that, we end up numbing the good emotions and experiences too.

The list of these ways of life goes on and on. Paul writes in Ephesians 4:31 about "bitterness and wrath and anger and wrangling and slander, together with all malice." He also mentions lying, stealing, and speaking ill of others. Being dead though alive and being children of wrath are things we all know to some degree, and some people know as most of their world.

God understands this. As we are hurt and feel we don't belong, we struggle to be or feel safe. We try day by day simply to be ok. We seek solace, protection, and solutions, and sometimes those solutions are rather less than life-giving. We live as children of wrath.

Remember from Chapter 4 about missing the mark? That's what being children of wrath ultimately is.

Resurrection, then, is going from being dead through trespasses (missing the mark) to being alive in a new way of life. This happens in small ways and big ways throughout our lives. God knows us, understands us, and loves us. God gives us this new life, healing us from the many deaths we face, and bringing us to the joys of resurrection life.

A New Way of Life:
Kindness, Tenderheartedness, Forgiveness, and Love

What then is this new way, this joyful resurrection life Paul writes about? Well, like the ways of life as children of wrath, the ways of resurrection life are also easy to understand; we do these things all the time as well. We act out of love. We forgive. We care about others. We let go our pride in order to have good relationships with others, rather than forcing our own way. We pause and rest. We see ourselves as part of a much larger whole, as part of a common humanity, and we honor our interconnectedness with one another.

The new life for Peter which I wrote about at the beginning of this chapter looked much like his old life. He was restored to being Jesus' disciple, living the love, forgiveness, and care of others that he had been living before his death in denying Jesus.

As a broad look at new life, Paul mentions three specific things: "Be kind to one another, tender-hearted, forgiving one another, as God in Christ has forgiven you" (Ephesians 4:32). Adding love to that mix, we end up with a way of life that is kindness, tenderheartedness, forgiveness, and love.

Some Ways of Resurrection Life

Choosing to act lovingly toward others, even when they anger us. Sometimes that is walking away from a fight or an argument. Sometimes it is simply listening to the others' pain (directed toward us as anger or contempt) and acknowledging their pain and how hard that is for them.

Forgiving and reconciling with others. "I was wrong" is a great phrase to keep handy. We are likely sorry, but admitting to being wrong does not require the other to feel badly for us, nor even to forgive us. Rather than seeking forgiveness, admitting to being wrong acknowledges the hurt we caused and honors the other. We can also be sorry and also express our regret. Admitting our fault, however (whatever that fault is), is a good first step.

Forgiving others as we hope they would forgive us is the other part of this. We choose to see others as hurt and broken people. Then we can see even the hurt they caused us through the lens of compassion.

Taking and making time to connect with others. We are social beings, meant and made for connection. In far-flung and disconnected societies, this can be hard, for introverts and extraverts alike. Some will have more connections, and some will have fewer. In whatever amounts, however, having and developing deep connections with others is an essential part of the way of resurrection life.

One way to do this is to spend time with a trusted group of people sharing deeply about our lives. This can be a group of friends who go out weekly, a small prayer group, an exercise group, or any shared interest group. Simply having fun with friends. There need not be anything religious about it.

Being at peace. This takes time and effort. Prayer and meditation are helpful. Finding a place of calm and stillness within the storms and uncertainties of life is key to a heart at peace. This is not simple passivity or choosing to be walked on. Instead, we work to act out of a place of peace and acceptance of what we can't control, rather than frantically trying to control that which we can't. From that place of peace, we can then act in healthy, healing ways, rather than harmful and destructive ways.

> O God of peace, you have taught us that in returning and rest we shall be saved, in quietness and in confidence shall be our strength. By the might of your Spirit lift us, we pray, to your presence, where we may be still and know that you are God; through Jesus Christ our Lord.[19]

---

19 A Prayer for Quiet Confidence, *The Book of Common Prayer* (New York: Seabury Press, 1979), 832.

Admitting powerlessness. Also essential is admitting powerlessness and giving up striving for control over others. Acceptance of the way things are, rather than constantly trying to make things be the way we want them to be, is part of the peace of resurrection life.

> God, grant us the serenity to accept the things we
> cannot change,
> The courage to change the things we can,
> And the wisdom to know the difference.[20]

No longer trying to improve the past. How often do we dwell on the past, mulling it over again and again, fantasizing about some way it could have gone differently? "If only," "what if" rerun memories are constantly playing in our heads. The challenge is, we can't actually improve the past. We can, however, accept it, learn from it, and find the blessings that have come from it, even from the bad parts. We can forgive. We can use our own mistakes and poor decisions to help others. We can turn the hurts of our past into blessings for others.

Doing with less and being content with who we are. Comparison with others is poison for the soul. Wanting more and more to feel that we are ok, that somehow all is well, is part of that poison. No amount of stuff can ever satisfy our needs for connection, acceptance, love, and worthiness. Things don't love us. In sufficient quantities, things can make us feel powerful or more successful than others (and therefore more worthy of love), but no amount of stuff can actually make us worthy of love. Also, contra proponents of the prosperity gospel, God's favor is not granted to us or shown to us by having lots of money and stuff. Jesus taught this truth:

> Do not store up for yourselves treasures on Earth, where moth
> and rust consume and where thieves break in and steal; but store
> up for yourselves treasures in Heaven, where neither moth nor
> rust consumes and where thieves do not break in and steal. For

---

20   Reinhold Niebuhr, *The Serenity Prayer,* 1933

where your treasure is, there your heart will be also (Matthew 6:19–21).

Therefore I tell you, do not worry about your life, what you will eat or what you will drink, or about your body, what you will wear. Is not life more than food, and the body more than clothing? Look at the birds of the air; they neither sow, nor reap, nor gather into barns, and yet your heavenly Father feeds them. Are you not of more value than they (Matthew 6:25–26)?

Our value does not come from our stuff but from the simple fact of our being. We are. We were born. We are children of God. In those simple facts lie our value and our worth.

Being generous. Another joy of doing with less and being content with who we are is that such a life can lead to generosity. With less fear and less need to hold on tightly for our own worthiness, we are free to be generous with others. With mutual and reciprocal generosity, we find that there is enough.

Spiritual Practices

Ultimately, everything mentioned thus far is a spiritual practice. Even so, there are some intentionally/overtly spiritual practices below which can be helpful ways of life.

> **Prayer.** Time spent in conscious contact with God. At the beginning, at the ending, and throughout your day—asking for help with your struggles; turning to God for peace and inspiration; seeking an outlook of acceptance, serenity, love, and service. Below are several forms of prayer:
> - Praying with knots or beads: Anglican Rosaries, Prayer Ropes, Prayer Beads, and many others are ways to pray which involve your hands (a tactile focus of prayer) and can incorporate repeated prayers as well as personal "in the moment" prayers.

- "Coffee Prayer": A time of quiet prayer and reflection in one's morning routine (it needn't involve coffee).

- A Daily Examen: Ending the day by offering all that is past to God, marking ways to improve, and celebrating things done well. The Daily Examen comes from the teachings of sixteenth-century priest Ignatius of Loyola. He believed the daily examen was a gift from God which can help us see God's work in all of our lives. Below is a simple daily examen which you can practice:
  - Open with prayer: "God, thank you for this day that is past; please grant me the serenity to see your presence throughout my life."
  - Then think through or write down the following:
    - Blessings and gratitudes from the day
    - Ways you succeeded and lived as you and God desire
    - Any failures, regrets, things you would have done differently or not done at all
    - Ask, "Where was God throughout my day?"
    - Where might God be leading you tomorrow?
  - Pray "The Lord's Prayer" (see below – Prayers for God's Will).
  - Conclude with a prayer like this: "God, I offer to you all of the day that is past; keep it for me that I may rest tonight in peace, and then, in the morning, give back to me that which I need, and hold for me that which I do not."

- Prayer for God's Will: Seeking to follow God's will and to align our own will with God's is not always easy, but it is a daily practice. We don't always know when we are following God's will, but we likely are doing so when we are calm and at peace with our decisions. Here is the prayer Jesus taught:

- Our Father, who art in Heaven, hallowed be thy name; thy kingdom come, thy will be done, on Earth as it is in Heaven. Give us this day our daily bread, and forgive us our trespasses, as we forgive those who trespass against us; and lead us not into temptation, but deliver us from evil.

Meditation. There are many forms of meditation which help to recenter us; to calm our bodies, minds, and spirits; and to ground us in God's presence. Some kinds of meditation are:

- Drawing mandalas, coloring, any form of drawing

- Taking a hike/walk

- Getting in the zone/flow of disconnecting from the stresses and noise of life

- Yoga, Tai Chi, and other forms of movement.

One form of meditative prayer is called "Centering Prayer." In Centering Prayer, you sit quietly, breathe slowly, and focus on the breath for 5–20 minutes, relaxing your body, and repeating a "sacred word."

The sacred word can be any word that brings you peace. During the meditation, as thoughts come clamoring for attention, repeat the sacred word in your mind, letting the thoughts go.

The point is not to rid your mind of thoughts but to practice letting the thoughts go and returning to the center, to the breath, to the presence of God in and around you in that moment. Over time, you develop a sense of calm and peace.

Listing & Sharing Gratitudes. Every day, write down three things for which you are grateful, no matter how large or small. Writing your gratitudes each day and sharing them with others helps refocus your mind and even rewire your brain to see more beauty and hope in the world. From that place, life's challenges are easier to face.

"The root of joy is gratefulness. It is not joy that makes us grateful; it is gratitude that makes us joyful."—David Steindl-Rast[21]

Reading Scripture or Other Healing Writings. Writings which focus you on healing, peace, and recovery: reading such writings, books, and daily reflections every day helps to focus and heal our minds and hearts.

Sharing Joys and Sorrows. Contact others; seek and give support— we are not meant to walk alone. Call a friend or neighbor. Make a practice of sharing your life, giving and receiving support with people you trust.

A Side Note about "Good Works"

In his letter to the Ephesians, in chapter 2 verse 10, Paul referred to these new ways of life as good works. He wrote that God made the good works for us, to be our way of life. These good works were a gift from God so that we might more fully know God, one another, and the connection, belonging, healing, and love for which we long, for which we were made.

With regard to Christianity, you may have heard about conflicts within Christianity between faith and works. This goes back to the protestant reformation in the sixteenth century. At that time, theologian John Calvin said that any good works, apart from being a Christian, are still problematic in God's eyes. We're completely corrupt, and yet God made good works. So, when we do good works, God sees the works and is pleased to see his handiwork, and yet displeased to see our corruption in them.[22]

---

21   David Steindl-Rast, *Gratefulness, the Heart of Prayer: An Approach to Life in Fullness* (Mahwah, New Jersey: Paulist Press, 1984), 204.

22   John Calvin, *The Institutes of the Christian Religion*, Book Three, chapter 15.3, accessed May 17, 2022, *Bible Study Tools, 2022*, https://www.biblestudytools.com/history/calvin-institutes-christianity/book3/chapter-15.html.

Seriously? Well again, God's sovereignty may be defended in Calvin's argument, but I ain't buying it.

God made these good works (think anything good anyone has ever done) to be our way of life. Well, of course he did. What didn't God make? Remember also that God made us in God's image. We are creators, as God is. We create good works in partnership with God. God made all good works, and God makes all good works with us. These good works are for us, with us, and a part of us.

When I read that God made good works for us, I see no flip side to that coin. I don't see that the good works are made wholly apart from us and are messed up anytime we come near them. The good works are good. Period. Anytime anyone does them, they are good. Period. These good works are part of who we are, and anytime we live them out, we are living as God created us to be. All of us—those of Christian faith, those of any faith, those of no faith—are living as God created us to be anytime we live out good works of love.

———————————

Passages from Paul's Letter to the Ephesians

Ephesians 2:1–10

You were dead through the trespasses and sins in which you once lived, following the course of this world, following the ruler of the power of the air, the spirit that is now at work among those who are disobedient. All of us once lived among them in the passions of our flesh, following the desires of flesh and senses, and we were by nature children of wrath, like everyone else. But God, who is rich in mercy, out of the great love with which he loved us even when we were dead through our trespasses, made us alive together with Christ—by grace you have been saved—and raised us up with him and seated us with him in the heavenly places in Christ Jesus, so that in the ages to come he might show the immeasurable riches of his grace in kindness toward us in Christ Jesus. For by grace you have been saved through faith, and this is not your own doing; it is the gift of God—not the result of works, so that no one may boast. For we are what he has made us, created in Christ Jesus for good works, which God prepared beforehand to be our way of life.

Ephesians 4:25–32

So then, putting away falsehood, let all of us speak the truth to our neighbors, for we are members of one another. Be angry but do not sin; do not let the sun go down on your anger, and do not make room for the devil. Thieves must give up stealing; rather let them labor and work honestly with their own hands, so as to have something to share with the needy. Let no evil talk come out of your mouths, but only what is useful for building up, as there is need, so that your words may give grace to those who hear. And do not grieve the Holy Spirit of God, with which you were marked with a seal for the day of redemption. Put away from you all bitterness and wrath and anger and wrangling and slander, together with all malice, and be kind to one another, tender-hearted, forgiving one another, as God in Christ has forgiven you.

CHAPTER 9

Healing the World from The Tribal God

"Lord, make us servants of your peace.
Where there is hatred, may we sow love;
where there is injury, pardon;
where there's despair, hope;"

—from a prayer attributed to St. Francis

I was in a Bible study the other day, and I heard someone talk about "the God of the Old Testament." This is a common trope among Christians. The story goes that the God of the Hebrew Scriptures seems angry and vengeful to Christians. The God of Israel fights for Israel and wins victory in war against other nations. He talks about his anger toward other nations, and, when Israel is turning away from him, his anger toward Israel. Christians hear and read these words of anger and vengeance, and God sounds scary. We tend to gloss over the parts about God's great love and the people's love for God.

Then, enter the Christian Scriptures, and Jesus talks about love and forgiveness. He heals people, and Christians tend to gloss over the parts about God's judgment . . . at least for them. In both cases, the God presented in the stories of scripture is being read as a tribal god. By this tribal reading, God is on our side, but may not be on yours. By this tribal reading, God is forgiving for us, and if you join us, God will be forgiving for you. As much as Christians talk about and believe that the God we worship is the God of the whole world (and indeed of the whole cosmos), we still often think of and pray to God as if he were a tribal god.

Here's an example. My father was in a Bible study/prayer group, and at one meeting, a leader asked, "How do you know God [the Christian god] is real?" One of the members then answered that he knew God was real "because the Allied Forces won World War II." My dad spoke up then, telling the group, "That dog won't hunt." He asked who they thought the German Christians were praying to throughout the war? Christians on both sides of the war were praying to the same God . . . or were they? What about Jews and Muslims fighting on different sides of the conflict? The names of the Gods were the same on both sides, but were all the people actually praying to different tribal gods?

This is tricky, because on the one hand, of course people of the same religion on different sides of the conflict were praying to the same God. Both were praying for safety for themselves and their families. Both were praying for victory. Perhaps God(s) did win victory for the Allied Forces, but that is a pretty tribal and narrow view of God. The Allied Forces might say God won because justice and freedom won. It did for some, but did it for all? Would all of the Axis powers agree? Throughout the long history of war throughout the world, has justice and freedom always been the winner in conflict? If not, or even if so, whose God won the victory?

People of the same religions generally believe in the same God, and yet when you bring conflicts over country, doctrine, and political affiliation into the mix, we quickly divide into our various tribes, looking to God to support us over them. This is a big challenge because we all desire what is right, good, and just. Of course we do, and so of course we believe God agrees with us. God must, therefore, be against the other side. So goes our logic.

Rather than look at the other side as those whom God is violently against, however, can we look with compassion on the other side? Can we realize that while God may not be for them on the issue at hand (and may we keep a healthy amount of uncertainty over that), God is still for them as beloved children?

For more on this idea, I offer the experience of Vincent J. Donovan, Roman Catholic missionary to the Masai people in Africa.[23] Sitting down with the people of one tribe, Fr. Donovan listened to their stories about themselves and about their God. They spoke of "Ingai," who was for the good, rich, and healthy people, and generally against the bad, poor, and sickly people. They talked about each tribe believing in their own tribal God.

After listening, he responded. He talked about Abraham, about God calling Abraham and telling him that he was the one, God over all the gods. The God of Abraham was the God of the whole world, not just of some tribes. He said there was no God who prefers some people over others, only the one God who loves all of humanity equally. There was a period of silence, and then someone asked Fr. Donovan if he had found the God over all the gods. Before answering, he considered the wars in which Christians prayed to their God for victory, and he realized that they too were praying to the tribal god. He said that he hadn't found the High God, and he invited the people with him to search for the High God together.

We are searching together for the High God, the God of All the Tribes. This doesn't mean we should renounce our religions. Of course we can continue to believe in God(s) as understood in our faiths. We can also accept the limits of our understanding, the limits of our faiths' understandings (or do we really think we can fully know and understand God?). Accepting these limits and uncertainties, we can love and believe in the faith we have, as it brings us to a greater understanding and awareness of God. We can love and believe in the faith we have as it brings us healing, connection, belonging, and love.

Notice that unlike with nations in conflict, mastery over others is nowhere a part of such a faith. People in conflict are often seeking mastery

---

23   Vincent Donovan. *Christianity Rediscovered*. New York: Orbis Books, 1982.

over others. As the people of Israel were being formed as a nation, for example (see Joshua, Judges, 1&2 Samuel), there were near constant conflicts with other nations. Who was going to win? Well, the nation with the strongest god, of course. As Israel would fight, God would win the victory over other nations' gods. So, the God of Israel was understood to be the supreme God over all other gods.[24] Even so, God was often understood as a tribal god. As with all the other tribal gods, God was seen as the God of Israel, not of all the peoples. He was God over all, but favored that one nation: a tribal God who sought to gain mastery over others, a concept to which we can still easily relate.

This mastery over others, however, is not the way of the church (nor ultimately the way of Israel). At the birth of the Church on Pentecost, Peter and the other apostles were gathered to celebrate the Festival of Weeks (Pentecost), as they had for many years before, but then, something strange happened. The Holy Spirit was revealed to them and to those gathered near them as tongues of fire, resting upon them. The Jews who had come from all over heard the apostles speaking to them in their native languages, not just in the Hebrew language. God was connecting these people from disparate parts of the region into one people, through the Holy Spirit. The revelation was that God was not just the god of one tribe, one people, but that God truly was the God of all the tribes, of the whole world, indeed of the whole cosmos.

On the birth of the Church at Pentecost, the apostles were not there to dominate others and force them into conformity. They were not meant to hold mastery over others. They were joined together as the Church to help bring greater unity to humanity through faith, hope, and love.

This idea had been spoken of through prophets to Israel many times before, and Paul wrote of this idea in his letter to the Ephesians. God is the God of all peoples and God's desire is for all of humanity to be united. In Ephesians chapters 1–3, Paul writes of the mystery of God that has been

---

24   We read in Psalm 82:1, "God has taken his place in the divine council; in the midst of the gods he holds judgment." Whether considered gods or lesser heavenly beings, they were all subservient to the God of Israel, the God of all creation.

revealed, namely, that God would gather up all things in Jesus, all things in Heaven and on Earth. Paul wrote of Jesus as sitting at the right hand of God in the heavenly places (where the other gods dwelt), and Paul wrote of the Church as the body of Christ, dwelling as Christ's body with God in the heavenly places right now, so that we are both here on Earth living out our mortal lives, and at the same time, we are in the heavenly places joined together as Jesus' body.

Paul went on to write that we are joined together with Jesus as part of God's revelation, that we are in the heavenly places revealing, even to the gods or heavenly beings, the unity that God has in mind for all of humanity. No more tribalism and no more tribal gods. One people living in unity.

Now, that does not mean that Christians are meant to convert all people to Christianity. We've tried doing that for a couple millennia, sometimes even forcing conversions on others. That's led to conflict, war, disunity, and atrocity.

Forcing, shaming, and coercing conversion has not been a quest for unity but the Church turning Jesus into one more tribal god. We don't find unity through tribalism and conflict. We find unity through love and belief that there is one God over all humanity (or not). Many of us call God by different names, and that's ok. God is big enough for all our names.

We don't need to be right in our beliefs, and we don't need other religions to be wrong. We can have unity and love with others while still having very different faiths. Throughout the Earth, we call God by different names, and God is big enough to answer to all of them. God's mission for the Church is to strive for unity among the peoples of the earth. God's mission for the Church is to live and to share God's great love for all humanity. God's mission for the Church is for us to be united, both here and in the heavenly places among the gods. Our mission, our way of life, is unity with all people through love and forgiveness, and to share that unity with all of humanity both here and in the heavenly places as God gathers up all things in him, both in Heaven and on Earth.

CHAPTER 10

LGBTQIA+ J

*"You keep using that word. I do not think it means
what you think it means."*

— Inigo Montoya, *The Princess Bride*

Throughout the centuries, the Church (both the people and the institution[s]) has done a great deal of good in the world. Ministries of healing during times of plague; huge amounts of charity work; offering hope in times of hardship and disaster; and proclaiming good news to folks dying to hear it, that they are beloved of God.

Unfortunately, the Church (both the people and the institution[s]) has also done a great deal of harm. While the people to whom this harm has been done are countless, the reason is often fairly similar. Fear.

Remember that much of Christian theology over the last seventeen hundred years or so has been based on or largely infected with fear. Will I or those I love spend eternity in torment? With such a question underlying so much of our theology, even those Christians who aren't actively afraid of Hell have that question permeating their beliefs / systems of beliefs. Further, that same fear has caused much reaction against countless groups of people who were/are seen as a threat to people's avoidance of eternal torment.

The reaction goes like this: I want to be sure that I will not be tortured forever, i.e., that I am "saved." Well, in order to be sure that I won't be tortured, I need to be classified among those who believe in Jesus and are saved. Obviously not all are saved (so such theologies go) because many don't believe in Jesus. Not even all those who do believe in Jesus are saved (so such theologies go), so I want to make sure I'm not like those who are on the outs with God.

Well, if I want to ease my mind that I am saved, and if that means not being like those who aren't, then I need a group of people whom I would classify as not saved. So, I need a group of people who are not like me!

Add to this various groups of people who, according to some of Paul's letters in the Christian scriptures, will not inherit the kingdom of God, and you've got a pretty easy recipe for Christians to classify groups of people as broken, damned, and most definitely not saved . . . unlike the ones who are saved, of whom those Christians are definitely a part.

While the lists of the damned, according to the "saved," are vast, I am going to focus on a particular group of people who have routinely been ousted by Christians. This group of people are beloved people made in God's image, and, at the time of this writing, they are finally getting recognition from the Church as being just that—beloved children of God, made in God's image. I am talking about the LGBTQIA+ community.

As a cisgender, heterosexual male, I can speak only as an ally, and I hope my thoughts will be helpful from that point of view. While I am attempting to write inclusively and correctly, I know I will make mistakes. I apologize for any errors made from ignorance.

Beloved Children of God

Every human being ever is a beloved child of God, made in the image of God. Every person who identifies as LGBTQIA+ is made in the image of God and is a beloved child of God. Tara Soughers, Episcopal priest and mother of two sons, one of whom is transgender, wrote a wonderful book about this fact, called *Beyond a Binary God: A Theology for Trans* Allies.*[25] In her book, Tara Soughers wrote about how gendered ideas of God not only limit our understandings of who is made in God's image but also limit our understandings of God.

One primary understanding of God that Soughers writes about is God as Father. This is scriptural and not a bad metaphor for God. It connotes many good qualities to God such as the love of an ideal father, the unity of family, etc. Such a metaphor for God can also have problems for many, such as those without a father figure or those with a terrible father figure. God as father can provide some healing in those cases, and God as father can also keep people away from an understanding of God as loving.

God as father need not be abandoned, but there are so many other metaphors for God, metaphors which do not limit God to a cisgender male, father figure, family man. The image of God goes so far beyond that of a cisgender male. Additionally, all genders along a spectrum of gender and all sexualities are a part of the image of God.[26]

Lesbian. Gay. Bisexual. Transgender. Queer. Intersex. Asexual. All are beloved children of God, made in the image of God, and the sexuality of all are blessed by God.

Addressing this truth of blessedness from a scriptural perspective, we can look at Genesis, to the beginning of the creation of people. In Genesis 1, in the first story of creation, the scripture writes that God made humanity male and female in God's image.

That means the image of God is both male and female and everything in between. Maleness and femaleness are not absolutes but are characteristics on a spectrum. Some might say that the absolute of being male or female is the presence of male or female genitalia, but not everyone is born with male or female genitalia. Some are born with both. Some are born with ambiguous

---

25   Tara Soughers, *Beyond a Binary God*, (New York: Church Publishing, 2018), 45–73.

26   Linda Tatro Herzer, *The Bible and the Transgender Experience: How Scripture Supports Gender Variance* (Cleveland: Pilgrim Press, 2016).

organs. They too are born in the image of God, with their genitalia just as it is. Their physical bodies are not mistakes and do not need to be corrected in order to conform to the image of God. They are beautiful people made in the image of God, and as such, we discover that God is all aspects of maleness and femaleness, not just ends on a spectrum.

Sure, We're All Children of God, but What about Sex?

In Genesis 1, after the man and the woman are made in God's image, they are told to be fruitful and multiply. Yes, this command to be fruitful and multiply does mean to have sex and make new, tiny humans. From that basic reading of scripture, many have argued that homosexual sex (or any sex which cannot make new, tiny humans) is the wrong kind of sex and goes against God's plan. Such a belief is rather shortsighted, however, in its understanding of scripture and of humanity and sex.

Procreation is one function of sex, but it is not the only function. Physical pleasure is another function of sex, or did no one notice that it feels good? Another function is the unity it brings to those who have sex: physical, emotional, and even spiritual unity. In *Living Buddha, Living Christ*, Thich Nhat Hanh wrote,

> "A sexual relationship is an act of communion between body and spirit. This is a very important encounter, not to be done in a casual manner. In our soul there are certain areas—memories, pain, secrets—that are private, that we would share only with the person we love and trust the most. We do not open our heart and show it to just anyone."[27]

Of course, sex doesn't always live up to those ideals, but such physical and spiritual unity, along with physical pleasure and procreation, is a function of sex. In all of those ways, sex is a part of God's command to "be fruitful and multiply."

---

27   Thich Nhat Hanh, *Living Buddha, Living Christ*, (New York: Penguin Group, 2007), 97.

Another aspect of "be fruitful and multiply" has nothing to do with sex. Being fruitful can also mean bringing about goodness and beauty into the world. Look at Galatians 5:22–23, where Paul wrote that the "the fruit of the Spirit is love, joy, peace, patience, kindness, goodness, faithfulness, gentleness, and self-control." In light of the fruit of the spirit, God's command to the man and the woman becomes, "Be loving, joyous, peaceful, patient, kind, good, faithful, gentle, and self-controlled, and multiply all of those ways of being. Bring ever greater love, joy, peace, patience, kindness, goodness, faithfulness, gentleness, and self-control into the world."

So, you see, "Have sex and make tiny humans" is one of the ways to fulfill God's command to "be fruitful and multiply," but it is far from the only way.

To those who would say homosexual sex is bad and wrong because it doesn't live up to "be fruitful and multiply," I would say, "yes it can, and yes it does." While homosexual sex can't result in the creation of new, tiny humans, neither can much heterosexual sex, or are infertile couples supposed to stop having sex because they are infertile? Of course not. Sex is a gift from God by which we get to make new, tiny humans, and by which we get to enjoy and honor each other. Even sex without the possibility of procreation is a way we can be fruitful and multiply, bringing ever greater love, joy, peace, patience, kindness, goodness, faithfulness, gentleness, and self-control into the world through the physical pleasures of sex and the emotional, physical, and spiritual unity of sex. That goes for heterosexual and homosexual sex.

A Further Look at Scripture

Many Christians would be against the above ideas and use other passages of scripture to say that homosexual sex is absolutely wrong, and scripture says so. So, let's look at those passages of scripture and see what they actually say. The Biblical scholarship addressing language for the next four paragraphs on

Leviticus comes from Dr. L. Michael White[28] (PhD, Yale) and a presentation he gave called "The 'H' Word: What the Bible Says about Homosexuality" at Palmer Memorial Episcopal Church in Houston, TX, in 2005.[29] At the time, Dr. White held the Ronald Nelson Smith Chair in Classics and Christian Origins at the University of Texas at Austin.

Looking first at two passages from Leviticus, we have:

- Leviticus 18:22 – You shall not lie with a male as with a woman; it is an abomination.

- Leviticus 20:13 – If a man lies with a male as with a woman, both of them have committed an abomination; they shall be put to death; their blood is upon them.

So, that's pretty strong language condemning men having sex with men, but let's look at why it is forbidden and what is actually being said.

Abomination seems like a pretty clear problem, but in Hebrew, in which the passages were written, the word means "abhorrent by reason of impurity." The act was seen as defiling the purity of the people, aka, doing their religion incorrectly. Considering that Leviticus is largely a book of temple regulations, which was likely written after Israel's exile to Assyria and Babylon (long after the time of the exodus and forty years in the wilderness, where the book is placed in the narrative of scripture), we see that these laws are mostly concerned with Temple regulations and purity of the Temple.

Other things listed as being "an abomination" were shepherds, lying, cheating in business, and burning (improper) incense. While men having sex with men is clearly prohibited in Leviticus, we can see that the prohibition is concerned with a particular understanding of a particular religion at a particular time. Coming after the exile, the priests in Israel wanted to make sure they kept pure and kept the nation pure to stay in God's good graces. The

---

28   White, L. Michael. L. Michael White. Accessed May 17, 2022. https://www.lmichaelwhite.com/.

29   White, L. Michael. "The 'H' Word: What the Bible Says about Homosexuality." YouTube. May 29, 2012. Accessed May 17, 2022. https://youtu.be/jraG8Xhounk.

idea was "If only we do our religion really, really well, and be good enough, God won't be angry with us, and our nation will be ok."

So, at that time, for the priests' understanding of the religion of Israel, men having sex with men was seen as impure. It was not necessarily, however, seen as a crime against nature. There were only two sexual acts which were described as crimes against nature, and they were bestiality and incest (Leviticus 18:23 and 20:12). Men having sex with men is not described as perverting God's created order. It is described as going against the religious purity and religious righteousness of Israel.

Even so, some would say sex between men is forbidden in scripture, so we must forbid it now. To them, I would ask, "Why?" There were 613 laws given in Torah, the first five books of scripture. Why is this particular law so important to Christians that it must be upheld when most of the other 613 laws of Torah are not?

Looking at later periods of scripture, God even declares through the psalmists and the prophets that he isn't overly concerned with the correct Temple worship and doing all parts of the religion correctly. More than proper religion, what God seems concerned with is people treating one another well.

Hear, O my people, and I will speak, O Israel, I will testify against you. I am God, your God. Not for your sacrifices do I rebuke you; your burnt offerings are continually before me. I will not accept a bull from your house, or goats from your folds. For every wild animal of the forest is mine, the cattle on a thousand hills. I know all the birds of the air, and all that moves in the field is mine. "If I were hungry, I would not tell you, for the world and all that is in it is mine. Do I eat the flesh of bulls, or drink the blood of goats? Offer to God a sacrifice of thanksgiving, and pay your vows to the Most High. Call on me in the day of trouble; I will deliver you, and you shall glorify me." But to the wicked God says: "What right have you to recite my statutes, or take my covenant on your lips? For you hate discipline, and you cast my words behind you. You make friends with a thief when you see one, and you keep company with adulterers. "You give your mouth free rein for evil, and your tongue frames deceit. You sit and speak against your kin; you slander your own mother's child.

Psalm 50:7–20

Day after day they seek me and delight to know my ways, as if they were a nation that practiced righteousness and did not forsake the ordinance of their God; they ask of me righteous judgments, they delight to draw near to God. "Why do we fast, but you do not see? Why humble ourselves, but you do not notice?" Look, you serve your own interest on your fast day, and oppress all your workers. Look, you fast only to quarrel and to fight and to strike with a wicked fist. Such fasting as you do today will not make your voice heard on high.

Is such the fast that I choose, a day to humble oneself? Is it to bow down the head like a bulrush, and to lie in sackcloth and ashes? Will you call this a fast, a day acceptable to the Lord?

Is not this the fast that I choose: to loose the bonds of injustice, to undo the thongs of the yoke, to let the oppressed go free, and to break every yoke? Is it not to share your bread with the hungry, and bring the homeless poor into your house; when you see the naked, to cover them, and not to hide yourself from your own kin?

Then your light shall break forth like the dawn, and your healing shall spring up quickly.

Isaiah 58:2–8

'With what shall I come before the Lord, and bow myself before God on high? Shall I come before him with burnt-offerings, with calves a year old? Will the Lord be pleased with thousands of rams, with tens of thousands of rivers of oil? Shall I give my

firstborn for my transgression, the fruit of my body for the sin of my soul?'

He has told you, O mortal, what is good; and what does the Lord require of you but to do justice, and to love kindness, and to walk humbly with your God?

Micah 6:6–8

God told the people of Israel time and again, "I don't care about how perfectly you do your religion. What I care about is how well you treat each other. Treat each other well, and that will be fulfilling the laws I have given."

As Rabbi Hillel said in the first century bce, "What is hateful to you, do not do to your neighbor. That is the whole Torah; the rest is commentary. Now go and learn." The purpose of the laws given was to make sure people did what was loving toward one another.

So long as the religious purity laws helped people to be more loving toward each other, they were well and good. If such laws began having the opposite effect, then they needed to be left undone in order to fulfill the purpose of the laws.

Now, some of the laws given in Torah seem obviously given to help people be loving toward one another. There are other laws, however, which seem to be given largely to uphold the correct practice of religion (as with ritual sacrifice, noted above).

Into which category did the law against men having sex with men fall?

For the most part, Leviticus 18:22 and 20:13 fall into the category of the correct practice of religion. Once such a law begins causing harm to people, preventing people from loving one another more fully, such a law should be broken in order to fulfill the purpose of the law.

By another reading of those texts, "a man lying with a male as with a woman" can have the meaning of forcible sexual violence by one man against another. So, men raping other men is forbidden, and such a prohibition obviously falls within the purpose of the law.

What about men having sex with men in a loving, committed relationship? What about men having sex with men in which the sex fulfills the purposes of sex: mutual pleasure and intimacy? What about when such sex helps bring forth the fruits of the spirit in the lives of those men? Is such sex forbidden by scripture?

No, it is not. In fact, such sex is not mentioned in scripture.

"Now, hold on," some would say. "Homosexuality is expressly forbidden in Romans 1:26–27, I Corinthians 6:9, and 1 Timothy 1:9–10." Is it, though? Again, we need to look at language, and again I am turning to scholarship from Dr. L. Michael White.[30]

In Romans 1:23–27, Paul writes:

. . . and they exchanged the glory of the immortal God for images resembling a mortal human being or birds or four-footed animals or reptiles.

Therefore God gave them up in the lusts of their hearts to impurity, to the degrading of their bodies among themselves, because they exchanged the truth about God for a lie and worshipped and served the creature rather than the Creator, who is blessed for ever! Amen.

For this reason God gave them up to degrading passions. Their women exchanged natural intercourse for unnatural, and in the same way also the men, giving up natural intercourse with women, were consumed with passion for one another. Men committed shameless acts with men and received in their own persons the due penalty for their error.

So, we have men seemingly having sex with men, and women having unnatural intercourse. Rather than the specifics of the sex acts (which aren't entirely clear), look at the reason Paul sees those acts as the wrong kinds of sex:

---

30   White, L. Michael. "The 'H' Word: What the Bible Says about Homosexuality". YouTube. May 29, 2012. Accessed May 17, 2022. https://youtu.be/jraG8Xhounk.

idolatry. Because of some people's idolatry, i.e., worshipping statues or other created images as though they were God, God gave those people up to non-heterosexual sex . . . because of idolatry.

What about people (and for the sake of this writing, centered on Christianity, Christian people) who have spent their lives worshipping and believing in Jesus? They aren't and never have been idolaters. They always have believed in Jesus, and yet, many have also always been homosexual. This is something different than what Paul was writing about, something not brought about by idolatry.

Additionally, Paul had a particular understanding of sex in his context. As a Jewish man, he believed in the laws of Torah and would likely, therefore, believe sex between men (and sex between women, maybe?)[31] to be ritually taboo. Considering that he was writing to an audience of Roman Christians, deeply influenced by Greek culture, he was likely addressing the common practice of men raping boys (they wouldn't have called it rape, but I will). The kinds of sexual activities Paul was talking about were very different from sex between consenting adults.[32]

If we look further at 1 Corinthians 6:9–10 and 1 Timothy 1:9–10, we find lists of sinful wrongdoers.

> 1 Corinthians 6:9–10 – Do you not know that wrongdoers will not inherit the kingdom of God? Do not be deceived! Fornicators, idolaters, adulterers, male prostitutes, sodomites, thieves, the greedy, drunkards, revilers, robbers—none of these will inherit the kingdom of God.

> 1 Timothy 1:9–10 – This means understanding that the law is laid down not for the innocent but for the lawless and disobedient, for the godless and sinful, for the unholy and profane, for

---

31 Sex between women is nowhere mentioned in scripture. "Unnatural intercourse" simply means nonvaginal intercourse.

32 I'm using the term "consenting" adults to be clear in my point. In actuality, any sex that is not consensual is not sex. It is rape.

those who kill their father or mother, for murderers, fornicators, sodomites, slave traders, liars, perjurers, and whatever else is contrary to the sound teaching.

Looking at the English words for sexual sins, we have fornication, adultery, male prostitution, and sodomy. Let's start with the easy one. Adultery is roundly condemned throughout scripture. Cheating on one's spouse, having sex with someone other than them, is a betrayal of the relationship between the married persons. Far from a simple purity rule which must be followed in order to appease a god obsessed with purity, adultery is forbidden because of the harm it does to the other person in the marriage, the harm it can do to the one with whom the adultery happens, and even the harm it can do to the adulterer. Adultery is choosing not to honor the other person in the marriage, but to disregard them and dishonor them.[33]

With fornication, male prostitution, and sodomy, Paul was probably not writing about what we may often think he was writing about. With fornication, we might think of having lots of sex with many different people. Such a practice is rife with potential hazards, including heartache, disease, making a new person when you're not ready to be a parent to that new person, etc. Such a way of living could certainly be warned against, and it may well be what Paul was writing about.

Just as likely, however, is that Paul was writing about pederasty. Male prostitution and sodomy were both included in that list, and "sodomy" is a word that didn't exist when Paul wrote his letter. The word he used would better be translated as pedophilia. Remember the context, a time and area where young men were commonly forced to serve as male prostitutes. In Greece, romantic relationships between grown men and young boys were common. Pederasty is likely what Paul was writing about, given the context of his writing

---

33   Realizing of course that sometimes, adultery is not done with total disregard for the other, but after years of a failed marriage, out of a place of deep grief and longing.

So Where Does That Leave Homosexual Relationships?

Homosexual relationships, as loving, mutual, committed relationships between adults, are not addressed (or possibly even considered) by Paul. When looking at the sexual prohibitions in scripture, we're looking at prohibitions against actions which cause harm to others. We're looking at actual harm done as with rape and pederasty. Harm done as a child being sexually assaulted by an adult.

What we're not looking at is harm done simply because someone is breaking a purity rule and upsetting God who arbitrarily said "no." Homosexual relationships are not condemned in scripture, and homosexual sex is not condemned in scripture. As with all relationships and all sex, it can be condemned when done in such a way as to harm another (rape, adultery, pederasty), but it is not condemned simply because it is taboo or because God has an arbitrary rule to follow. It is not condemned in order to make people pure enough for God.

Relationships between homosexual couples are blessed by God. Sex between homosexual couples is blessed by God. Homosexual sex and homosexual relationships fulfill God's command to be fruitful and multiply. They bring about physical, emotional, and spiritual unity. They bring the fruits of the spirit. Lesbian. Gay. Bisexual. Transgender. Queer. Intersex. Asexual. All are beloved children of God, made in God's image, and the sexuality of all are blessed by God.

CHAPTER 11

God as Trinity, God as Mother, and How This All Fits with a Credal Faith

"As truly as God is our Father, so truly is God our Mother."

— St. Julian of Norwich

So, I've written some things in this book that might be rather different than what you're used to hearing about Christianity, but what I've written is hardly revolutionary. In fact, everything I've written fits within a credal faith. The primary creed or belief statement of the Church is the Nicene Creed. It is called the Nicene Creed because it was formed during a church council in an ancient Greek city called Nicaea in the early fourth century.

Bishops from throughout the church gathered to hash out what the church ultimately believed, primarily what they believed about Jesus. Was he God? Was he human? Was he a good blend of the two, or something else entirely? By the end of the council, they finally agreed upon the understanding of Jesus as fully human and fully divine. Then they worked out language to state this truth as clearly as possible.

The creed was added to over the centuries at other full councils of the church and through that process, we have the Nicene Creed as it is today:

We believe in one God,

the Father, the Almighty,

maker of heaven and earth,

of all that is, seen and unseen.

We believe in one Lord, Jesus Christ,

the only Son of God,

eternally begotten of the Father,

God from God, Light from Light,

true God from true God,

begotten, not made,

of one Being with the Father.

Through him all things were made.

For us and for our salvation

he came down from heaven:

by the power of the Holy Spirit

he became incarnate from the Virgin Mary,

and was made man.

For our sake he was crucified under Pontius Pilate;

he suffered death and was buried.

On the third day he rose again

in accordance with the Scriptures;

he ascended into heaven

and is seated at the right hand of the Father.

He will come again in glory to judge the living and the dead,

and his kingdom will have no end.

We believe in the Holy Spirit, the Lord, the giver of life,

who proceeds from the Father and the Son.

With the Father and the Son he is worshiped and glorified.

He has spoken through the Prophets.

We believe in one holy catholic and apostolic Church.

We acknowledge one baptism for the forgiveness of sins.

We look for the resurrection of the dead,

and the life of the world to come. Amen.

Taking a look, you can see that there is nothing about what I've written about salvation or Jesus that contradicts anything in the Creed. My understandings are different than some others' understandings, but that doesn't make them non-credal. There is a lot of room in the creed for different understandings and beliefs within the Christian faith.

Ok, you may ask, but what if someone believes something that doesn't quite square with the Nicene Creed, or what if someone has a hard time believing something that is in the creed? Well, notice the first word of the creed. "We."

"*We* believe . . ." This is the church's faith, and *we* as the Church do believe this. Some may have a hard time believing certain parts of the creed, but others in the Church are there to believe it for them. Then at another time, those roles may be reversed. There have been plenty of times when I have been in doubt over much or even most of the creed, but Sunday after Sunday, I could still proclaim that faith because *we* still believed it, even when *I* didn't.

If you want to believe, but you have a hard time with parts of the faith, that's ok because *we* still believe it. The faith of the Church is a communal faith, not an individual one. Christianity is, after all, a religion of community, not a religion of individuals. By God's very nature, God is a community of persons, and Jesus always taught that his Church was a group effort, not an individual activity.

If you have uncertainty about the faith, realize that it is the Church's story, not your own. Then, you can choose to believe the story, to accept the story, to relinquish some control and let your story be part of the story of Jesus. You can let the belief be real enough to change your life, even if it doesn't make sense.

God as Trinity

Now regarding this Trinity idea, you'll notice there are three sections to the creed. One about God as Father, one about God as Jesus, and one about God as the Holy Spirit. The trickiness of the triune (three in one) faith is this: "How can God be three persons if God is one?"

Well, on the one hand, that is kinda tricky, on the other hand, not so much. See, in scripture, God is said to be one (Deuteronomy 6:4, John 2:19). So, there is only one God.

God is said to be Father (Isaiah 64:8, 1 Corinthians 8:6, Luke 11:12). Easy enough, the one God can be understood to be God the Father. (Though remember from the previous chapter, that "Father" is only one among many metaphors for God.)

Here's where it gets tricky. Jesus is also said to be God (John 1:1, John 10:30, Colossians 1:15–17). So, God became human as the person, Jesus, but Jesus calls God "Father." Now we've got God as Father and God as Jesus, the Word of God, which is also God, which spoke creation into existence. And God is one. So, God is Father, and God is Son. Confused yet? Good. So am I.

Then, the Holy Spirit is understood to be God (Psalm 51:11, 1 Corinthians 6:19, Luke 3:22). At Jesus' baptism, we see the Holy Spirit descend upon Jesus, the Son, as we hear the voice of God the Father saying, "This is my son, the beloved, with whom I am well pleased" (Matthew 3:17). We now have all three persons interacting together, distinct from each other, and we're still saying there is one God?

Yup. That's exactly what we're saying. There is one God, and we understand that God to be a communion of persons.

How does that work exactly? The short version is, "Who knows?" It is a mystery beyond our understanding, and yet we believe it to be true. While it is difficult to wrap a logic bow around the idea, the beauty and deep truth of God as community makes quite a lot of sense.

Think in terms of relationship. Throughout creation, we find relation-ship. In animals and plants, we find ways in which life happens together. God, by God's very nature, is relationship, and we are made in God's image. So, think of the closest relationship you have. The more you know someone and the more love you share, the greater unity you have with that person. Now, think of someone you've never met, never heard of, and never will have any relationship with. I'm guessing you find less unity with that person.

Now, take away the limits of physical creation, multiply that greater unity with those you love by infinity, and the unity of the Trinity might start making some sense. Three persons bound so perfectly together in love that they are one. They always were, always are, and always will be. God is by God's nature the love of persons in relationship: three united as one. One God. Three persons.

So, Is God a Dude?

So again, the first named person of the Trinity is God the Father. Then Jesus is God the Son. Finally, there is the Holy Spirit. That does seem a bit male-cen-tric as an understanding of God. It does not, however, make God male.

The Holy Spirit is not given a gender. She can be male, or he can be female.

Jesus, of course, was a male, but when he was resurrected, Jesus became anyone and everyone. Looking again at Matthew 25:31–46, we see Jesus telling people that whatever they have done to others, they have done to Jesus. That means women as well as men. That means transgender people as well as cisgender folks. That means intersex and asexual people as well. Jesus became the every-person, as God dwells in all of us.

Now regarding God as Father, that is rather decidedly male. Those in scripture who spoke and wrote of God, wrote primarily of God as male, and Jesus spoke of God as "Father." Can God, then, be understood as Mother? Of course, she can. God is all genders, so calling God "Mother" is perfectly understandable and even scriptural.

God as Mother

How can we understand God as mother? Many have wondered this. Remember, Genesis 1:27 says, "God created humankind in his image, in the image of God he created them; male and female he created them." God created all of humankind in God's image, male and female. That means that there are both male and female aspects to God.

While most of scripture does view God as male, there are passages of scripture which indicate the female nature of God.

- "As a mother comforts her child, so I will comfort you" (Isaiah 66:13).

- "Wisdom is radiant and unfading, and she is easily discerned by those who love her, and is found by those who seek her" (Wisdom of Solomon 6:12).

- "For she is a breath of the power of God, and a pure emanation of the glory of the Almighty; therefore nothing defiled gains entrance into her. For she is a reflection of eternal light, a spotless mirror of the working of God, and an image of his goodness" (Wisdom of Solomon 7:25–26).

Wisdom has long been associated with the Holy Spirit, God as woman.

God as mother is also seen in Jesus' talking about Jerusalem. "How often have I desired to gather your children together as a hen gathers her brood under her wings, and you were not willing" (Luke 13:34)!

God as mother is not a commonly written understanding of God in scripture, but that just means that most of the folks who wrote the scriptures understood God as male or God as father. Such an understanding is by no means exhaustive (can God really be fully defined by words in a book?), and the images of God as woman and mother in scripture are not erased by their paucity. They need not be overshadowed or swept aside. They should be celebrated.

God is woman just as much as God is man. God is male, female, and every gender in between. God is mother just as much as God is father. We are all beloved children of God, and unless I'm mistaken, children most generally come from a mom. As much as God is our dad, God is our mom.

Healing. Connection. Belonging. Love. That is what we are most after in our lives. God as mother can bring us that, just as God as father can.

A Word from Juliana of Norwich

Juliana of Norwich, or Julian of Norwich, lived from 1342 to approximately 1416. She was an anchoress, one who devoted her life to prayer and solitude. She lived as an anchoress in St. Julian's Church in Norwich, England, and it is by this church's patron saint that she is called "Julian." Her given name is unknown, as is much of her life. What we do know of her comes from her writings, a portion of which is below. During times of plague, famine, and poverty, Juliana of Norwich gave counsel, love, and hope to people in need. The passage below is from her writing, *Revelations of Divine Love*.

God is Our Mother

From *Revelations of Divine Love*, by Juliana of Norwich (1342–1416), (LIX, LXXXVI).[34]

> *It is a characteristic of God to overcome evil with good.*
>
> *Jesus Christ therefore, who himself overcame evil with good, is our true Mother. We received our 'Being' from him and this is where his Maternity starts. And with it comes the gentle Protection and Guard of Love which will never cease to surround us.*
>
> *Just as God is our Father, so God is also our Mother.*
>
> *And he showed me this truth in all things, but especially in those sweet words when he says: "It is I".*

---

34 Juliana of Norwich, *Revelations of Divine Love*. Accessed May 17, 2022, *The Holy See*, https://www.vatican.va/spirit/documents/spirit_20010807_giuliana-norwich_en.html.

As if to say, I am the power and the Goodness of the Father, I am the Wisdom of the Mother, I am the Light and the Grace which is blessed love, I am the Trinity, I am the Unity, I am the supreme Goodness of all kind of things, I am the One who makes you love, I am the One who makes you desire, I am the never-ending fulfillment of all true desires. (. . .)

Our highest Father, God Almighty, who is 'Being', has always known us and loved us: because of this knowledge, through his marvelous and deep charity, and with the unanimous consent of the Blessed Trinity, he wanted the Second Person to become our Mother, our Brother, our Savior.

It is thus logical that God, being our Father, be also our Mother. Our Father desires, our Mother operates, and our good Lord the Holy Ghost confirms; we are thus well advised to love our God through whom we have our being, to thank him reverently, and to praise him for having created us and to pray fervently to our Mother, so as to obtain mercy and compassion, and to pray to our Lord, the Holy Ghost, to obtain help and grace.

I then saw with complete certainty that God, before creating us, loved us, and his love never lessened and never will. In this love he accomplished all his works, and in this love he oriented all things to our good and in this love our life is eternal.

With creation we started but the love with which he created us was in him from the very beginning and in this love is our beginning.

And all this we shall see in God eternally.

CHAPTER 12

Healing. Connection. Belonging. Love.

*I'll journey on and bear my load,
'cause light on the horizon comes.
Travelling this forgotten road,
light on the horizon comes.*

– "Light on the Horizon"

So, going back to the beginning, I wrote this book for the hurt, the blessed, and the damned. That pretty well covers all of us. All of us are hurt to varying degrees and in a variety of ways. All of us are blessed, whether we feel it or not, and all of us are beloved children of God. Finally, all of us have at one time or another felt rather damned. I don't mean eternally sentenced to torture. I mean we've all felt forsaken, cast aside, desperately in need of healing. This book and the faith it represents is written for all of us.

All of us need healing. All of us need connection, belonging, and love. Healing from our hurt and brokenness is, in fact, what helps us to live and experience the connection, belonging, and love we all desire.

That very healing is what God intended for us by becoming human. That healing is what Christianity is all about, so that we can live lives of connection, belonging, and love. As Jesus himself said, "I came that [you] may have life, and have it abundantly" (John 10:10).

Jesus' purpose was to heal us, not to condemn us, and certainly not to frighten us like the bogeyman. Jesus was God, connecting with us physically in all aspects of our humanity. Every part of our humanity is blessed. Every part of our humanity is united with God. We don't always use our humanity in particularly blessed ways. Instead, we often use our humanity to hurt others and ourselves, leaving us feeling damned. That all stems from our hurt and our brokenness. God understands that, hence God's desire to bring us healing.

The abundant life Jesus came to bring us is life in which we can live without shame[35] or fear. According to researcher, entrepreneur, and bestselling author Dr. Brené Brown, "Shame is the intensely painful feeling or experience of believing that we are flawed and therefore unworthy of love and belonging."[36] We all feel shame, and in the darkness of isolation and judgment, shame grows, and we become more and more hurt. We lash out and hurt others. We bottle things up and isolate ourselves even further. We seek too much to please others and deny our own right to be.

In these and many other ways, shame leads to some of the greatest hurt we feel and cause. Shame tells us we don't belong. Shame keeps us from connecting to others. Through that disconnection, we end up feeling even more like we don't belong. Shame tells us we are broken and damned.

The antidote to shame, Brené Brown has found, is empathy: compassion and understanding. That is exactly what God has given us in becoming human.

"Life is hard," God says.

"I get it. I've lived it. I understand the pain and hurt you feel, and I understand why you hurt others out of that pain. I understand the shame you feel, and I have become one with you so that you may come to believe that you are never alone. You are

---

35   See Brené Brown's writings on overcoming shame through living wholeheartedly – Brenebrown.com

36   Brené Brown, *Daring Greatly.*

never unworthy. You never don't belong. You may be broken, but you are not damned. You are loved, and you belong, both to me and to each other."

That healing, that connection to God and one another, brings an assurance of belonging and love. That is exactly why God became human. Not to condemn. Not to make afraid, and not to shame. God came to heal us of our shame so that we may have life and may have it abundantly.

Shame has no part in the abundant life God brings.

Guilt, on the other hand, does have a loving role to play in abundant life. Guilt tells us we have done wrong, and we need to make amends. When we mess up, we need to help heal the harm we have caused. That's what love does. Love brings healing, and guilt is a part of that love. Nothing that we have done, however, needs to bring us shame. Shame is not a tool God uses. God seeks healing, connection, belonging, and love, the total opposite of shame.

So, may you find healing. May you grow in connection, belonging, and love. May you help bring healing to others, that they too may grow in their connection, belonging, and love.

That goes even (and maybe especially) for those who seem to be your enemy. Jesus taught us to love our enemies and to bless and pray for those who harm us (Luke 6:27–36). That doesn't mean we let folks stomp all over us. That isn't love. You get to defend your right to be, and at the same time, you get to look at the other with compassion. You get to see with the eyes of God into the hurt of that person which is the cause of the harm they have done to you.

You also get to look deeply into yourself and determine what your part may have been in the conflict. It may be very small, but looking into our own hearts for our parts in conflicts is a part of love.

You may not be able to fix or correct the other person, but you can work with God to bring greater healing to yourself—healing so that you do not treat that other person with retribution or resentment, bringing about greater harm and shame for them. Even if justified, retribution and resentment are poisons which you give to yourself while trying to hurt your enemy. Letting go and releasing the hurt of the past helps to release resentment. Acknowledging one's own part in the conflict, however small, is also part of releasing the resentment so that healing can take place within your heart, radiating out from within your soul to all beyond you.

As the Psalmist prays, "Create in me a clean heart, O God, and renew a right spirit within me. Cast me not away from your presence, and take not your holy Spirit from me. Give me the joy of your saving help again, and sustain me with your bountiful Spirit" (Psalm 51:11–13).[37] May the words of this Psalm bring you healing, and may this prayer be always in your mind, on your heart, and near your lips, that you may be a minister of healing.

As ministers of healing, we ask God to restore our own hearts, and we see that the hurts of others are also our own hurts. The healing we need is also the healing they need. We are one even with our enemies, just as God is one with us. In that unity is healing. In that unity is God's incarnation.

May God's incarnation, God's joining with humanity, bring you compassion and understanding to overcome any shame or estrangement you may feel. That is the purpose of Christianity, to heal us of shame and disconnection and to lead us to abundant life.

I encourage you to further explore your faith, and if the ideas of Christianity in this book resonate with you, seek out others to live this way together. That may be in a church community, and it may start with a group of friends. If after gathering with friends for a while, you want to explore the faith further in a church community, I encourage you to go together. Try some communities out for a time. You may hit and miss before finding a faith or a community that truly connects with you.

I can personally speak for the Episcopal Church, that it is a church in which people are generally able to explore, to wonder, and to question

---

37   Book of Common Prayer version, *Book of Common Prayer* (New York: Seabury Press, 1979), 657

together. People are generally welcome to come as they are. The presence of the Nicene Creed means that people in the church get to explore and question their faith because "we" still believe the church's faith. At the same time, the Episcopal Church is not monolithic, and it will not be the best path for everyone. That's the beauty of so many denominations and different expressions of Christianity within those denominations.

Also, as you seek a community to live out your faith with others, realize that even in the best church communities, there will be people who drive you nuts (to put it mildly) and people whom you will drive nuts. I encourage you to give and receive grace. Give and receive compassion, understanding, forgiveness, healing, and love. The Church is a bunch of screwups. It is a collection of people who are in need of healing and who have found that healing through Jesus, through the incarnation of God, and through the teachings and way of life that Jesus gave.

Remember, there are no individual Christians. The way of Jesus is the way of community, just as the nature of God is a communion of persons. That communion, that love and belonging, is what God intends and hopes for us. That communion is why God became human, to heal us so that we may share in the communion of love that is God. May these words bring you healing.

May God bless you and keep you.

May God's face shine upon you be gracious to you.

May God's face shine upon you and grant you peace.[38]

On Faiths Other than Christianity

Many find healing, connection, belonging, and love through Christianity, through God becoming human.

38　Numbers 6:24–26 (Author's paraphrase)

Many do not.

Many do, however, find the same healing, connection, belonging, and love through faiths other than Christianity, and many find the same without faith in any god at all. If Christianity, even as presented in these pages, ends up not bringing such healing, please explore other faiths that may.

While I cannot speak to the healing, connection, belonging, and love that people find through other faiths or ways of life, people of those faiths can. Talk to folks of other faiths. Try those faiths out. Explore, and see if there is a faith that that does bring you healing.

The next several chapters, while limited, are intended to give you a start in exploring other faiths (or in one case, atheism, rather than faith). I've had interviews with people of other faiths (friends and friends of friends), and in their stories, they tell of the healing, connection, belonging, and love their faiths have given them.

If one of their stories resonates with you, I encourage you to further explore that faith. As with my advice for exploring Christianity you may want to explore a faith with others, with a group of friends. Realizing that no faith is monolithic, try some communities out for a time. You may hit and miss before finding a faith or community that truly connects to you.

Keep searching. Search with others. Believe that you are beloved of God. Know that none of your hurts, nor the harms you have caused, makes you damned. You may have some amends to make, as do we all, but that is part of healing. We seek to heal as we are healed. We seek to bless as we are blessed. We seek connection and love as we then grow in both and share them with others.

We are broken, and we are blessed. May you find healing, connection, belonging, and love, and may you be a blessing for others.

Blessings and peace be upon you,

Brad+

PART II

STORIES OF FAITHS OTHER THAN CHRISTIANITY

CHAPTER 13

Annie & Judaism

Rabbi Annie and I have been friends for over a decade, and she is one of my heroes. In about 2010, we were both part of an interfaith clergy group, so when I decided I wanted to learn more about Judaism, especially first-century Judaism, I asked Annie if we could meet for coffee and talk about faith. This led to our friendship, which I treasure to this day. As you read below, please note that what follows includes some mystical experiences which Annie had, and living the practices of Judaism helped lead to these experiences. This is Annie's story, however, and is not intended to describe or speak for all of modern Judaism. For an introduction into Jewish ideas, Annie suggests https://www. myjewishlearning.com/.

Would you begin by stating what your beliefs are, the basics of your faith? For example, you wrote the following in your biography for Temple Sinai. Could you expand on these?

What I believe most strongly is that all people are made b'tzelem Elohim, in the image of God. Because of this fundamental belief, I recognize the image of God in everyone—regardless of race, sexual orientation, religion, or background. I strive to honor the holiness in each person and greet them with openness and kindness.

I am truly in love with Judaism and its teachings; I look forward to the struggles our tradition demands, and I rejoice in the ways it uplifts my life. Judaism has the power to move us, change us, and shape our lives.

Brad,

Here are my answers to your questions. I have been percolating on them, and I hope they are answered in the fullness you need. However, I need to begin with a rather big caveat. Here goes.

You know I had this intense and magical mystical experience a couple of years ago. I felt as though I was swimming in God's love; the molecules separating us started to dissolve and I felt connected to everyone and everything. I felt like a channel, giving voice to something that was not me. It was intoxicating, amazing, and life changing. I knew we were all connected to one another and to Source. And I came away knowing just a few things for sure: The only things that matter are giving love, receiving love, and creating safe spaces for others to give and receive love. That's it.

After this experience, the Jewish clothes that had always fit so comfortably started to feel constraining. They just did not fit as well because I recognized all the ritual for what it was—just pathways to reach that pool of love.

I could not invest myself in the existential questions that so captivated the Jewish community anymore. Jewish survival was not critical to me.

The fixed times of prayer . . . eh. All of it just became secondary to expressions of LOVE.

This was definitely challenged; don't get me wrong . . . the ideal is often hard to live. But this was how I felt in my soul, and still what I feel. And it is part of the reason why I cannot stay a congregational rabbi. It is no longer as authentic an expression of my soul as it once was.

I have found more expansiveness and connection with thinkers like Byron Katie and Eckart Tolle and Martha Beck and people like THAT than in any of the thinkers, or books, or classes I have taken with Jewish thinkers.

I just cannot get myself that worked up about the things they care SO MUCH ABOUT. I don't know how to explain this well, but that is where I am. Hebrew is still my love language to God, and Judaism is still my path—I don't think that will ever change. But I guess I don't see the path as the purpose anymore.

So, all of that is to say, I don't think I am the best rabbi for you to speak to anymore to give you a sense of what Judaism is.

When you ask me what my beliefs are, my beliefs are Jewish, but they're also not Jewish in some ways. I am a mystic, to be sure, and just as likely to be inspired by Christian mystical teachings as Jewish ones. That is not technically kosher for us Jews! And as long as it is love, I just do not care about what is or is not kosher anymore.

I guess those are my beliefs, but they are not the basics of "my faith," if you assume my faith is Judaism. My beliefs are that this world is all illusion:

We create our reality in many respects.

This world is a womb for our souls, and our souls will be born into a world we cannot imagine.

Our entire purpose is to live in freedom, joy, and love, and to swim in a constant current of these things, endlessly giving and receiving them.

I believe we are infinitesimally small, that we matter not at all, and that we are also the entire universe in and of ourselves. I think all time is always happening. I believe that everything will be okay in the end, somehow someway. I believe that God is an unchanging, unending flow of Love that permeates all things, and that we can change our actions through religious or spiritual practices to open ourselves to more of that flow, or we can make choices that keep us further away from that flow.

But the Flow of Holy Love is ALWAYS there for us, no matter what we do or have done. We can always step into it.

The issues of punishment and justice and judgment are not God's issues—those are human issues, based not on love but on fear. Love knows that punishment is not necessary, ever. I believe all life IS created in God's image; in other words, we are all created with sparks or drops of that holy flow of love within. It is what draws us toward one another; it is what draws us toward that feeling of something greater than ourselves.

Those sparks—those droplets of holy flow—are in EVERYTHING. So, when I was swimming in God's love, I truly loved EVERYONE. I was in love with everyone. And that meant I was in love with myself, and nature, and the world. It was just exquisite. And while I do not feel that way now, I sometimes have glimmers of it, on the other side of absolute certainty, that anything is true.

These are my beliefs. Are they Jewish beliefs? Some of them may be. Some of them are not. Do I still believe that Judaism has the power to shape us, change us, etc.? Yes, I do, because if it were not for this path I would not be here today. I am grateful that Reform Judaism does not demand absolutes—that would never have worked for me. The process of questioning, engagement, struggle, ownership—I do love all of that.

My wife teaches religion at an Episcopal school and teaches about religions other than Christianity. When learning about Judaism, she had the students tell about the Torah, and a Jewish student said the Torah was like a good friend he could talk with over and over. Does that resonate with you?

The Torah . . . I love the image that the Torah is a good friend. Beautiful. I think Torah, like prayer, is all metaphor. I think it is a recording of a meeting with Source that was so powerful the echoes of that meeting continue to reverberate to this day—that is something powerful, holy, unique.

I think Torah is also a mirror. We are taught, turn it, turn it, for everything is in it. That teaching from Ben Bag-Bag (or Ben Hei Hei?) in Pirkei Avot[39] is supposed to be this lesson that we can find everything we need in

---

39   Joshua Kulp. *English Explanation of Pirkei Avot.* Accessed September 8, 2022, Sefaria. https://www.sefaria.org/English_Explanation_of_Pirkei_Avot.5.22.1?lang=bi&with=all&lang2=en

the Torah. Like the student said, a good friend we can continue to speak with forever, basically.

But what I have found, in these many years of engaging with Torah lovingly, is that if I come to Torah with the attitude that it has something to show me, I always am shown something. If I come to it with the attitude of "this is ancient, I will never find anything," then I don't. When I am in an angry place, I find anger. When I am in a place of love, that is all I see in the text.

Entire stories have transformed before my eyes because I came at them with a different understanding, and so that is why I say it is a mirror. As with any long-term relationship, the way we engage with Torah shows us things we may not want to see about ourselves. Do we trust that process? Do we trust the text?

The greatest lesson I ever learned about Torah is to never assume I know more than the text. It has allowed me to approach it with humility and the knowledge I always have more to discover—so that is what happens.

I've written about a deep longing we all have for God—"For God alone my soul in silence waits; from him comes my salvation." How have you experienced that longing, and how has it been fulfilled for you in Judaism?

Regarding the longing for God, I understand that. I have never felt so lonely in my life as when that feeling of swimming in God's love ended. Oh! That was terrible. Honestly terrible. Very lonely and alone-feeling.

I have come to trust, though, that as with every relationship, there are times of deep connection and intimacy and then times when I need my space. I need time to do work, to write, to learn, to grow. I have a plaque in my office that says, "Hands to work, hearts to God," and that is the way I feel most of the time. I just try to keep my heart and spirit open to the flow, and when I don't feel it strongly, I know it will come. Eventually.

I have loved all of our conversations about faith, life, the universe, and everything. You helped me to see how much more my faith has to do

with this life than life after death. That's a greater focus of Judaism, and at one point, you described it as releasing the light (a mystic teaching of Judaism?). Will you tell about the aspect of Judaism bringing light, love, and healing into the world?

So . . . Judaism, while definitely having a concept of the world to come (many concepts, actually!), has never made that the main focus of our faith. Judaism instead focuses on this world, and in some ways transforming THIS world into "olam haba"—the world to come.

I love this idea. I think that IS what we need to do! The mystics of the fifteenth to sixteenth centuries elevated this idea with their cosmology. They believed that when God created the world, God's presence was so strong it filled everything and there was no room for anything else. So, God made an action called "tzimtzum," or contraction—God contracted into Godself and that left space for something else.

God then created light (first day, all that good stuff!). The mystics, though, say this light was SO BRIGHT that it too would not allow any other part of creation. So, God created vessels—keilim—to hold the light. The light embedded itself into the vessels, which then shattered and made their way into the rest of creation that God had made—the world, all matter, US.

That is also why God created humanity—to give us a mission to repair all that is broken. That is called TIKKUN OLAM, repairing the world. The mystics believed this was why God created JEWS, not just humanity, but I think we can be expansive. :) They also believe the tikkun, the repair, occurred from correct performance of the mitzvot—correctly lighting the Shabbat candles, for example, or correctly getting dressed in the morning.

That is why so many Jews, to this day, care so much about the CORRECT way to observe Jewish law—they believe it REALLY, REALLY matters in the sense of tikkun olam, repair of the world—and also repairing the supernal light of creation, and uniting God with Godself. Today, I think we can understand it this way AND understand it more broadly. Humanity was created with a mission and a purpose—we are partners with God in creation and repair—and it is our job to heal this world and make it heaven on earth.

This mystical theology, by the way, deeply influenced my personal theology. The flow of Source—that is all Jewish mysticism. The sparks in each of us—that is also Jewish mysticism. The way I deeply diverge from it is that I do not think the goal is to correctly perform the mitzvot (fear based) but to do right action and speak right words (am I Buddhist?) to allow us to draw closer / step into the flow of Source. I am just a mishmash. And I am totally okay with that. I do not need to fit into a system—I am just me.

I love you so much, friend!

Annie

CHAPTER 14

Inaya & Islam

Inaya is a physician who works in internal medicine, and she and I share a mutual friend. It was our friend who introduced us so that I could have this interview about her faith. We began texting to arrange how best to hold the interview, and we chose email. What follows below is our email correspondence, interview Q&A, and follow-up.

Brad:

Hi, Inaya, and thank you again. The purpose of these chapters is to give people some glimpses into other religions than Christianity. My goal is to offer folks healing, connection, love, and belonging, and while I find that through Christianity, many will not. I can't speak to other faiths, but I want to offer a bit of a jumping-off point so folks can explore other faiths if they want to.

While an interview with an individual is hardly a full introduction to another faith, it is not meant to be. The chapter is meant to be human stories of faith (not comparative religion), ways of sharing what others have found in their faiths.

Inaya:

Brad, I really enjoyed reading your book's introduction. Your ideas on Heaven & Hell really resonated with me, as my faith has me believe something similar. I appreciate you letting me share Islamic ideologies to tie us together, instead of drive us apart.

Would you begin by stating what your beliefs are, the basics of your faith?

My religion is Islam, which literally translates to "peace." I consider myself Muslim, which translates to "one who submits (to God)." The basic tenets of Islam are simple. It is a monotheistic faith, where we only worship God. Allah is merely the Arabic word for God. We believe he is the same God of Adam, Moses, Noah, Jesus, Muhammad, etc.

We only worship God. We view Adam, Jesus, etc., and even Muhammad, as Prophets, sent to spread the word of God. We do not worship or pray to any prophet, including Muhammad. We believe in Adam–Eve & Satan, Noah & the Ark, Moses & the Pharaoh, Mary being a virgin mother to Jesus, Abraham & his sons, David & Solomon, etc. In fact, Jesus is the most mentioned prophet in the Quran. He is beloved in Islam but not viewed as a son to God.

Our holy book is the Quran. In it are the divine words of God. There is only one version of the Quran. It is in Arabic and remains unchanged since its revelation nearly fourteen hundred years ago.

Muslims follow five pillars of Islam, which are believing in one God with Muhammad as his last prophet, praying five times daily, fasting in the month of Ramadan, giving charity, and performing the religious pilgrimage of Hajj.

Did you grow up in the Muslim faith, or did you convert to it? What kept you or brought you to the Muslim faith, and are Healing, Connection, Belonging, and Love something of what you have found in your faith?

I was born into Islam, but my husband converted from Christianity. What drives my faith is the idea of an ever-merciful God. A God that loves us regardless of our human flaws. One that does not need any mediator to intervene between us and him. He gives this amazing but sometimes cruel world a point. I believe there is a Heaven. I have felt God in many high and low points in my life. He guides me in my daily life and helps me with my calling as a physician.

CHAPTER 15

Lukas & Atheism

Lukas and I have known each other for years. When we met, we were both Christians in the same church. Then, over time, Lukas became an atheist. Though he went from believing in God to not believing in a god, his basic views on life and people have not really changed. He is a deep thinker, and I am blessed to call him a friend. What follows is a combination of email correspondence and notes from an in-person interview we had.

Would you begin by saying what your beliefs are? Realizing you do not believe in a god, what do you believe in?

Right off the bat, my response to this one is that you're gonna have to be more specific. Like most people, I believe a lot of things about a lot of topics. I believe I exist. I believe pineapple can absolutely go on pizza if you want it to. I assume this question would normally be about religious beliefs, but I don't really have a lot of those. I guess the religious beliefs I do have are things like religion should be separate from the state, and that people should be free to practice any religion or lack thereof in any way that does not infringe on other people's rights.

It seems like asking what my values are, where they come from, or how I believe it is possible to know things would be more to the point.

My core values are:

- All humans are intrinsically valuable.

- We are responsible for our own actions.

- We all have to live together, and when push comes to shove, we all have to make it work.

- I was confused by forgiveness for a long time. Ultimately, I realized the release of forgiveness is for oneself, even more than for the other person.

- I can be mad, want accountability, and acknowledge it wasn't ok. Then I can release it.

How do you get through hard times without a belief in God (a question often asked by Christians)?

My counter question is, "How does a belief in God help you through hard times?"

For me, getting through hard times is largely through relationship with other people. I don't need an idea of God or resurrection to think things will get better or to have a willingness to adapt. That just seems how life works. As near as we can tell, we exist to keep the chemical processes of things going. It seems in the nature of life to keep living. I don't feel a need for God for that to happen.

Like the original existentialists, I encountered this question in the negative first: going through difficult times and not being able to reconcile that with a loving God. I could probably reconcile that more now.

The basic question is, "If God is all powerful, then why doesn't God stop the bad stuff?" God doesn't do so, therefore, God either does not care or God cannot stop it. So, either God doesn't exist, or God is evil. I would prefer to believe God doesn't exist.

You grew up Christian. What didn't work with Christianity for you? What was missing?

The short answer is execution, as in how it's done (not as in nailing people to trees). I have no problem with Jesus or his message, but I do have a problem with a lot of his followers.

The longer answer is that Christianity has spent several hundred years as a powerful institution. To go back to the first question, I have come to believe that any religion practiced by a majority of people within a place will inherently become a tool of oppression. I can go on about why I think that and what exactly I think that means, but in the interest of staying on topic, as a queer person in America believing in social justice, education, and freedom of thought, I am not willing to call myself a Christian or to frame my beliefs through the church. No offense :)

My problem was less of the "see you in hell" doctrine and more the dogmatic approach to morality. Follow these rules and don't question them and that is what it means to be a good person. It seems like applying your own morality to someone being more important than whether or not they are hurting anyone. A behavior may be hurting no one, but because it goes against the rules of morality, you're seen as a bad person.

That's tied to the idea of scaring people into good behavior, supposedly being loving and affirming to someone, but not respecting their free will.

Do you find no longer being a Christian to be liberating? Are there parts of the faith or parts of the religious practice that you miss?

Again, I need to preface this by reiterating that I respect you and your right to have a faith, but leaving has brought me nothing but joy. I do think it's been liberating, in a fairly literal sense. Deciding not to draw my ethical beliefs from a list of books that hasn't been updated for hundreds of years has given me a lot more freedom to explore different ways of thinking, freedom from a dogma.

Obviously, it's also given me the freedom to choose what I believe, rather than trying to interpret an absolute truth. I value both of those freedoms. I do feel like I want more spiritual practice in my life, but I don't particularly miss Christian religious practice. I do love requiems and gothic cathedrals, but that's more from an art history standpoint.

Since leaving, I've taken up hatha yoga more seriously (originating as a Hindu religious practice) and found that I love it and its philosophy. I might potentially be interested in a faith. I don't know. What really interests me is the human aspect of spiritual practice, not the divine aspect of spiritual practice.

We were talking over coffee one time, and I asked about ethics. For many people of faith in a deity, the beliefs of their faith help guide them into moral action (hopefully to treat others well). You referenced the writings of Simone de Beauvoir, saying moral behavior (treating others well) stems from the basic idea that we all have to live together. Can you say more about that?

Ok, seriously though, I guess I'll start by picking apart the question.

First, I'd like to draw a distinction between morality and ethics, since you've used both words for what looks like the same concept. I don't know a complete history of the distinction off the top of my head. Within the context of Western/European philosophy, the concept of morality has existed in religion at least since the arrival of Christianity. The concept of ethics has existed at least since Kant, although I think it might be older. I haven't read a lot of Kant—I don't like him.

As an existentialist, Beauvoir drew heavily from ideas popularized by Nietzsche, who was adamant about the distinction between morality and ethics. Basically, his distinction is that morality is a culture's rules governing acceptable behavior; so when he wrote about good and evil, he was referencing morality. Morality didn't necessarily have anything to do with ethics, or a more detached idea of actions that hurt people versus actions that help people. Part of why philosophical writing, including my own, is so dense is that we make normal words mean absurdly specific things.

Anyway. Beauvoir explicitly wrote a book on ethics, not morality, and in her book, she discusses how you could possibly know how to act without divine guidance and moving forward from a morality that had resulted in World War II.

So, now that I've clarified the question, I can start answering it.

In the immortal words of Spiderman, "With great power comes great responsibility." For Beauvoir, great responsibility comes from great freedom. She writes:

> However, far from God's absence authorizing all license, the contrary is the case, because man is abandoned on the earth, because his acts are definitive, absolute engagements. He bears the responsibility for a world which is not the work of a strange power, but of himself, where his defeats are inscribed, and his victories as well. A God can pardon, efface, and compensate. But if God does not exist, man's faults are inexpiable.[40]

Basically, what that passage means (or what I take it to mean) is that if we do not assume there is something more powerful than we are, something that could fix our mistakes or undo our successes, we are responsible for whatever outcomes we create. There is no one coming to help us clean up our mess, so we had better figure it out on our own. I think what I said about all having to live together was a summary that doesn't really do the idea justice—if we create the world, we are responsible for the world we create.

So, if I want my bedroom to not have trash all over the floor, I am responsible for picking up any trash that is there and for not putting any more trash down. But I don't just live in my bedroom. I live on a planet with seven and a half billion other people in it. Even if I still only think selfishly, I want

---

40   Simone de Beauvoir, *Ethics of Ambiguity,* Accessed May 17, 2022, *Reddit, 2014,* https://www.reddit.com/r/philosophy/comments/23s1tv/how_well_does_simone_de_beauvoirs_ethics_of/.

a world where I will not be murdered, where I will still have a planet to grow old on, where my loved ones are safe and happy. So, it is my responsibility to create that world by behaving in ways that bring it about.

I wrote in the introduction about wanting to offer Healing, Connection, Belonging, and Love in the pages of this book. I assume you are looking for those same things in life. How do you find them? What is the source of those things for you?

Like I talked about in the last question, I think connection is unavoidable. You can choose to fight every single human being in the world, or you can work together. Even if you had to explain that to a computer, I think the math is hard to argue with. I don't think you need to put it in those terms, though. I think all of those attributes are essentially and naturally human, so much so that it makes more sense to ask how we ever lose them than how we find them. We're not solitary animals. Even in our physical forms, we're optimized for different tasks. It takes at least two people to make another person. It takes a lot more than that to survive. As much as we tend to "other" those we see as different, it's hard not to believe that some level of empathy, however limited, is hardwired, if not into everyone, then into enough people.

I was going to write something more explanatory, but when I sat down to do it, all I could think of was the lengths we go to trying to rationalize what we seem to intuitively know about how to treat each other. I think that covers connection, love, and belonging, at least in the abstract sense.

If you were asking how I find those things outside of a religious community, I have a group of friends that regularly meets to play tabletop games. We've been virtual since the pandemic and will likely continue to be now that we've all graduated. I'm familiar with the concept of a third place, which doesn't have to be a place of worship; that group is mine.

I don't believe that human beings are inherently good and that bad people are only that way because something has corrupted them. But I do think that connection, love, and belonging are the rule rather than the exception.

CHAPTER 16

Jax & Heathenry

Jax and I have been friends for over twenty years. She is one of my personal heroes, and I am honored to have her be a part of this book. I called Jax's faith "Heathenry" because that is the name she gave for her faith. It is a reconstructed faith in the Norse Pantheon: reconstructed because very few still believe or practice the faith. Jax studied and began practicing the faith years ago, based on her research and the stories of the Edda. Below is our email interview correspondence and follow-up questions.

Would you begin by stating what your beliefs are, the basics of your faith?

My most fundamental belief is that there's no way for anyone to truly know what's out there—if there is a god or other higher power(s) or what happens after death. Each religion has books, stories, traditions, and/or teachers that they can point to in support of their faith, but that's faith in a book, story, tradition, and/or teacher. Because it's impossible to know what's true, no loving or just deity would punish people for inaccuracy.

The way I see it, then, each person who finds a calling toward faith, religion, or spirituality, instead of searching for truth, would do best to find the framework that gives them joy and helps them be the best version of themselves. I don't think there are right and wrong faiths, though there might be faiths that are right or wrong for a particular individual, and the right faith for one person will be the wrong faith for somebody else. Any faith that makes you stronger, kinder, and live your life more fully can be the right faith for you.

I've chosen to refer to myself as a Pagan, though at the moment I'm not practicing regularly. I have a Heathen-ish outlook, which is the Germanic/ Norse bent of Paganism. I think of my religion more as a practice than as a faith. While some Pagans believe literally in their gods, other Pagans think of them more as spiritual entities that derive power from collective use—as in, they have power because we give them power through our belief—or even simply as parables, archetypes, and/or metaphors for natural phenomena. For me, what exactly they are isn't important. What is important is that practicing my faith brings me peace and gives me joy.

When I'm active, my primary practice is venerating my ancestors and spirits of the land—the history leading to me alongside the space that I currently occupy. Ancestors to me are not just blood relations but include anyone who helped form the foundation I came from. This practice helps me be grateful for who came before me and for the blessings currently in my life. It also reminds me that my actions have consequences both for the land around me and for the future, even long after I'm gone.

In Heathenry, this concept is called "wyrd"—the idea that we're all connected, not just in the world today but through time as well. None of us are responsible for the whole tapestry, but we're all responsible for our stitch.

I also like to celebrate the turning of the year and generally follow the Wiccan Wheel of the Year because it makes sense and breaks the year up into manageable and meaningful chunks. Holidays for me are a way of checking in on where I'm at in my life and for contemplating different topics of what it means to be a good person. For example, at the fall equinox, I tend to focus on what it means to find balance and how letting go of unneeded things and outdated thinking can help me be a stronger, more loving person.

You grew up Christian. What didn't work with Christianity for you? What was missing?

Christianity is a big religion with a lot of variances between denominations, so to give some context to my experiences below, I was raised in a mainstream Protestant church in a small town in the South.

Also, before I get into this, I want to reiterate that I think everyone needs to find what works for them. My issues with Christianity are specific to me and my experiences. Other people will have completely different experiences, and I fully support anyone who chooses Christianity to help them be a better, stronger, kinder, and more loving person. Even after changing faiths, I still look at Jesus as an example for how to live a good life.

So, okay, here goes. I read your introduction (which was just lovely, by the way), and what you said about the concept of Christians go to Heaven and everyone else goes to Hell was actually what kickstarted my conversion. I would ask questions like "What about people who were raised in a different faith?" and "What about people who never heard about Jesus?" and generally received answers like "Everyone gets an opportunity," like everyone gets their own road to Damascus event.

Even if it's true that everyone on Earth somehow learns about Christ (which doesn't seem likely to me), here I was being *raised* in the church that gets you to Heaven, but somebody who'd heard of Jesus *one time* was going to have their eternal soul judged by the same standard as mine? How can we say God is just and loving, then suggest he made such an unfair system? I know now that not all Christians believe in salvation through faith, but that was the tradition I was steeped in growing up and, in my experience, is a pretty common version of the faith—that being a Christian is what gets you into Heaven.

While I was still a church-going Christian, I got into quite a number of arguments with people that revolved around this in-group/out-group mentality. My beliefs that Christians aren't better or worse than other people were not well tolerated. Now, as a convert, it's still my experience that a lot of Christians treat me differently when they find out I'm not one of them, particularly if they find out I converted out. Not all Christians, of course! But this tribalism also isn't uncommon.

It's important to me to have a faith where nobody cares what religion you are, and nobody cares if you convert out. If somebody was Pagan and isn't anymore, I don't care. Their journey doesn't affect me in any way and their decision to leave doesn't change my opinion of them. What really matters is being a good person, and being a good person isn't tied to which religion you ascribe to.

Another issue was the lack of female representation. The main female figure is a virgin mother, which isn't an archetype that resonates with me. Of course, there are a number of strong women in the Bible, like Deborah, Esther, and Magdalene, and most religions around today were founded when misogyny was the norm. Most faiths overrepresent men; this isn't just a Christian issue but a human history issue. However, I wanted a faith that was trying to find more balance, something I didn't see growing up. (My church had a female assistant pastor, and while some people embraced it, there was a lot of "she should be raising her kids, not leading a church" sort of talk as well.)

To add to that, I also saw other people, like members of the LGBT+ community, treated with not just a lack of representation but with disdain and even abuse. When I was young, I was taught that anything in the LGBT+ spectrum was a sin. But as I grew older and started interacting with a more diverse population of kind, loving, good people across the spectrums of gender and orientation, many of whom had been deeply traumatized by a church or by church members, I realized how just flat-out wrong that persecution is, and I didn't want to be part of it.

I know discrimination is not a fundamental part of what Christianity has to be, and I know Christians who respect all people regardless of faith, gender, orientation, etc. But, well, you asked what didn't work or what I was missing that prompted me to convert, so . . . yeah, frustration with tribalism was the root of it.

How did you come to come to believe in Heathenry? You were searching for something in a long journey of faith. What did you find in Heathenry?

I've always had a feeling that there's something out there that's larger than human understanding, and when I left Christianity, I still wanted something, some system of faith, that connected me to that greater power. Paganism with its variety and sense of whimsy and wonder appealed to me immediately. And, of course, I appreciate the female deities. Paganism is not very structured, welcomes everyone, has almost no dogma, and requires doing a lot of research on your own, all things that appeal to me.

I love the basic principle of the Wiccan Rede: "An' it harm none, do what ye will." It's surprisingly tough to live a life that harms none—every shopping trip is suddenly fraught with thinking about how my purchases affect the community of the world, not just me and my family's budget. It's challenged me to live a more sustainable and more equitable life when I remember that my choices have far-reaching consequences that aren't always obviously apparent. I also appreciate that it defines morality by how it affects myself and others. If no one's getting harmed, then it's fine—there are no rules for the sake of rules.

Heathenry, in particular, I was drawn to because my family hails from that part of the world. I love the Norse myth of the world beginning with the collision of fire and ice; I love the symbolism of the world tree, Yggdrasil, that all the worlds hang from. I love the crazy stories of Loki, Freyja, Odin, etc. But most of all, I draw inspiration from the story of Ragnarök. The gods know they're going to fail and they're going to die, but they go fight anyway. Life is about the struggle—fighting for what's right and for authenticity—and the outcome isn't as important as the journey.

As someone who's always thinking about and planning for the future, that reminder to be brave and live in the now is good for me. According to the Havamal, the wise sayings of Odin, "Cattle die and kinsmen die, and so one dies one's self; one thing now that never dies, the fame of a dead man's deeds." No matter what happens after life, what we did while we were here remains. What we do with our time on Earth matters because it carries on beyond us. It's all about wyrd.

I wrote in the introduction about wanting to offer Healing, Connection, Belonging, and Love in the pages of this book. Are those things something of what you have found in your faith? Please explain.

Some yes, some no. Maybe I'm a little odd, but the lack of rigidity or even common beliefs makes me feel more deeply connected to other people. Knowing that the person next to me has different experiences, different learning, and different interpretations makes me feel free to be my own authentic self without worrying if I'm crossing a line or offending some- one with my "heretical" ideas. On the other hand, this lack of common- ality doesn't promote the same sense of belonging that I used to feel in the Christian church. I used to sing in the choir and teach VBS, and there are things about that strong community and my place in it that I miss. I attended a Unitarian Universalist Church for a while and it gave me some of that, but I was a new mother at the time and my new responsibilities got in the way. For the most part, since leaving the church I've found my sense of community in other ways.

I never really thought about it until you asked this question, but the Christian church traditionally was responsible for so much of a community's lifeblood—the healing, the aid, the social outlet, the connection that people couldn't otherwise get in a more isolated world. I wonder if I didn't have as many options for connecting with others, would I be more tempted to hide my beliefs and attend church to have access to that? But now I get my sense of community from my writer community and my friends, not my faith. I get love from family and friends. I get my healing from therapy and from individual practices, like meditation and tarot, that are more psychological than spiritual. (Some people practice tarot as a magical activity, whereas I look at it more as a way to stimulate my thinking with archetypal imagery—less magical and more a brainstorming tool.)

I guess I just don't expect my faith to provide me with these things. For me, spirituality is an end in and of itself, more of a bonus experience than a necessary part of leading a fulfilling life.

In reading about your faith at one point, you wrote, "I believe in Odin. Like, for real." That hit home with me in a major way. For me, Odin was a myth. We'd been taught in school (briefly, very briefly) about "Norse Mythology." Then I read that what was mythology for me was faith for you. I realized then, the obviousness that what was faith for me was mythology for many others. My faith could be taught as "Christian Mythology." Seeing your faith in something I had thought of as myth helped me see my faith as more real because I was able to see it also as myth, and therefore as, well, faith. Hmmm, ok, I'm not sure there's an actual question there, more of a thank-you, and what is your reaction to that?

Aww, you're such a lovely person! Writing that piece was tough because it felt like opening myself up to ridicule to say I believe in a myth. But what you said right here is why I wrote it. Religion, no matter what you practice, requires a leap of faith, and each of us has the same right to take that leap in the direction that calls us. Personally, I think believing in nothing is also a leap of faith—it's a choice just like everyone makes. What really matters isn't what you choose to (or not to) believe in, but what your belief leads you to do with your life.

You are one of my heroes for all of the above. Thank you, Jax. You helped me find a faith within Christianity that brought me healing and love, not fear. Sharing with me your journey of faith helped me find the healing, connection, belonging, and love for which I had been longing within my own faith.

You are one of the first people I told about my conversion. I am, I think, the only person I know who converted out of Christianity and told a Christian first. But I knew you and I knew you were the kind of person who would love and accept me anyway. You have always been a light, and you are one of the people that I bring to mind whenever I see people claiming to be Christians while picketing a funeral or other such nonsense. Honestly, you're one of the main reasons why I still believe in the goodness of Christianity. Thank you for that. Thank you for showing me (without a single lecture or sermon) that the church I grew up in and loved very dearly has the potential for a bright, kind, loving future of doing good in the world.

CHAPTER 17

Buddy & Taoism

Buddy and I met through a mutual friend, and I have loved our conversations and getting to learn from him. He is a businessman, father, podcaster, and spiritual seeker. His book, Powerless but Not Helpless: A Meditation Book of 81 Verses from the Tao Te Ching, *looks at how the verses of the Tao fit and work with the 12 Steps of recovery.*

Would you begin by stating what your beliefs are, the basics of your faith/ philosophy?

I have given up attempting to figure out who, what, when, or where God is. Today I think of God as "what is" in this moment. When Moses asked God who he was, God said, "I Am Who I Am." God said he was present tense, not "was" or "will be." If God is in the present moment, that reinforces the principle of God being Love. I can only give and receive Love in the present moment; my fears take me out of the moment and into yesterday with regret and resentment or tomorrow with worry.

As a result, the way that I approach God has changed. My approach to God has actually flipped. I used to think that first I believed, then prayed in faith, then changed, and then I could love others. I have experienced the opposite. When I take the action of loving others, whether I believe it will work or not, I change. It actually has nothing to do with what I believe or if

I believe at all; it has to do only with taking action. I've found that if I chose to love instead of making a fear-based decision, I am loved in return and experience God. Whether this love comes from a person or from within as a result of making an effort, I always experience love (God).

My experiences in alcohol recovery brought about this revelation. Here are two quotes from the book *Alcoholics Anonymous, Fourth Edition*:

Practical experience shows that nothing will so much insure immunity from drinking as intensive work with other alcoholics. It works when other activities fail. Page 89[41]

"If you have a resentment you want to be free of, if you will pray for the person or the thing that you resent, you will be free. If you will ask in prayer for everything you want for yourself to be given to them, you will be free. Ask for their health, their prosperity, their happiness, and you will be free. Even when you don't really want it for them and your prayers are only words and you don't mean it, go ahead and do it anyway. Do it every day for two weeks, and you will find you have come to mean it and to want it for them, and you will realize that where you used to feel bitterness and resentment and hatred, you now feel compassionate understanding and love. Page 552[42]

Did you grow up Taoist? What kept you or brought you to Taoism?

I was brought up Christian in a Southern Baptist home in the south. As a teenager, I attended a charismatic church that changed my life. I had an authentic experience with God that still influences my life today.

I started drinking socially in my late twenties and eventually began drinking more to reduce business stress. It was not long before I was a daily

---

41   *Alcoholics Anonymous*. 4th ed. (New York, NY: Alcoholics Anonymous World Services, 2001), 89. https://www.aa.org/the-big-book

42   *Alcoholics Anonymous*. 4th ed. (New York, NY: Alcoholics Anonymous World Services, 2001), 552. https://www.aa.org/the-big-book

drinker with a problem I could not control. I sought God fervently using every tool at my disposal that I had learned while being a Christian for over twenty years but was not successful.

Through five brutal years of multiple relapses and coming to the point of suicide, I was able to surrender enough to let the program of AA work. Based on these experiences, I knew something was missing in my beliefs concerning God.

I researched Buddhism, other Eastern religions, and Gnostic Christian writings. As I studied different belief systems, I found this story of the Vinegar Tasters (based on the painting by the same name). This painting describes a metaphorical meeting between Confucius, Buddha, and Lao Tzu. These are the three men credited for founding the three major belief systems in China: Confucianism, Buddhism, and Taoism, respectively.

The three men tasted vinegar by dipping their fingers in a vat, which was common in China during this period. Each man's reaction demonstrated his philosophy of life.

- **Confucius spit out the vinegar.** He asked, "Why would anyone taste something so vile?" Confucianism comprises rules of conduct to correct moral decay and degeneration. Much of China today still follows many of Confucius's teachings, similar to the Old Testament Book of Proverbs.

- **Buddha swallowed the vinegar and suffered through the taste.** He stated life is full of suffering. Just as he suffered through the taste of the vinegar, we suffer through life due to our desires and attachments.

- **Lao Tzu tasted the vinegar and smiled.** Lao Tzu smiled, not because the vinegar was pleasant, but because it tasted just as it should taste— acceptance! Lao Tzu accepted the vinegar for what it was, already perfect—not needing his approval, disapproval, or effort to correct or fix in any way.

This painting reminded me of the story "Acceptance Was the Answer," in the book *Alcoholics Anonymous*. The more I read about Taoist philosophy, the more I saw the application of principles I had learned in recovery. I started seeing AA slogans like "All Is as It Should Be" and "Let Go and Let God" demonstrated in numerous Taoist texts.

I knew I had found what I was looking for in Taoist philosophy. The Tao Te Ching (pronounced Dow-De-Ching) is second only to the Bible in global publication.

Through years of studying Taoist philosophy, I have found a practical spirituality that has helped apply the 12 Steps in all areas of my life, especially surrendering more of my will and life's cares.

I wrote in the introduction about wanting to offer Connection, Love, Belonging, and Healing in the pages of this book. Are those things something of what you have found in Taoism? Please explain.

Taoism's primary text is the Tao Te Ching—loosely translated as "The Book of the Way of Virtue." I thought Taoism was about balance, but I have found it to be more about the flow of virtue that encompasses everything.

All through Taoist literature, we see our needs met when we meet the needs of others. Taoist philosophy is about accepting the moment for what it is. Rather than always thinking about ourselves and conniving to advance, we advance by helping others advance. Very simple but not easy. Since Taoism is over twenty-five hundred years old, many application examples involve nature.

Humility

The supreme good is like water, which benefits all of creation without trying to compete with it. It gathers in unpopular places. Thus, it is like the Tao. *Tao Te Ching, Verse 8, J. H. McDonald*[43]

---

43   *Tao Te Ching*, translation by J. H. McDonald, accessed September 8, 2022, Microsoft Word – Tao Te Ching – trans. by J. H. McDonald, https://www.unl.edu/prodmgr/NRT/Tao%20Te%20Ching%20-%20trans.%20by%20J.H..%20McDonald.pdf.

Forgiveness

After a bitter quarrel, some resentment must remain. What can one do about it? Therefore, the sage keeps his half of the bargain but does not exact his due. A man of virtue performs his part, but a man without virtue requires others to fulfill their obligations. The Tao of heaven is impartial. It stays with good men all the time. *Tao Te Ching, Verse 79, Gia-Fu Feng*[44]

Guidance

Do you have the patience to wait till your mud settles and the water is clear? Can you remain unmoving till the right action arises by itself?

The Master doesn't seek fulfillment. Not seeking, not expecting, she is present, and can welcome all things. *Tao Te Ching, Verse 15, Stephen Mitchell*[45]

Providence

Every step is on the path. *Lao Tzu*

I've written about a deep longing we all have for God—"For God alone my soul in silence waits; from him comes my salvation." How have you experienced that longing, and how has it been fulfilled for you?

I did not have to give up Christianity. I regularly see Christian beliefs in my Taoist readings. Taoist philosophy complemented what I had learned of Christianity rather than opposed it.

I experience God through the fruit of the Spirit: Love, joy, peace, patience, kindness, generosity, faithfulness, gentleness, and self-control. I was taught that the fruit of the Spirit is Love and the rest are manifestations

---

[44]   *Tao Te Ching*, translation by Gia-Fu Feng, accessed September 8, 2022, Tao Te Ching – Lao Tzu – A Comparative Study, https://www.wussu.com/laotzu/laotzu79.html

[45]   *Tao Te Ching*, translation by Stephen Mitchel, accessed September 8, 2022, Terebess Asia Online (TAO). https://terebess.hu/english/tao/mitchell.html#Kap15

of Love. If God is Love, then when I experience the fruit of the Spirit, I am experiencing God. I can only experience the fruit of the Spirit (Love) and in turn, God, in this moment.

Learning to live in the moment is a lifelong practice. Other than humans, the rest of nature lives in the moment. Living a life of Love and daily meditation is the tool I use to experience God daily. I "sit with" whatever is disturbing me until I can see what action is needed to find acceptance. I have found peace waiting in the most unacceptable situations when I accept the moment for what it is, not by trying to change it to what I want. I have experienced God more through accepting the seemingly unacceptable than at any other time. Only after accepting the moment for what it is can I determine whether there is anything I need to work to change.

There are two affirmations I use for accepting the unacceptable:

1. Thank you for everything. I have no complaint whatsoever.

2. I would not change _____ even if I could.

These are difficult statements that, in the beginning, are usually stated from a place of unbelief. Belief is not necessary, but action is. I used these tools to find peace as my son was dying at the age of twenty-five. The peace I found through acceptance is the closest I have come to experiencing God.

I also experience God as I Love others and experience Love in return. I look for ways to insert Love and understanding into every interaction. If I am spiritually fit, I look for a way to be helpful rather than manipulate a situation. All of life is a mirror; I always receive what I give.

PART III

SERMONS: LEARNING FROM JESUS' LIFE AND TEACHINGS

CHAPTER 18

Advent Sermons

Prisoners of Hope
1 Advent, Year C
December 2, 2018

"There will be signs in the sun, the moon, and the stars, and on the earth distress among nations confused by the roaring of the sea and the waves. People will faint from fear and foreboding of what is coming upon the world, for the powers of the heavens will be shaken. Then they will see 'the Son of Man coming in a cloud' with power and great glory. Now when these things begin to take place, stand up and raise your heads, because your redemption is drawing near."

Then he told them a parable: "Look at the fig tree and all the trees; as soon as they sprout leaves you can see for yourselves and know that summer is already near. So also, when you see these things taking place, you know that the kingdom of God is near. Truly I tell you, this generation will not pass away until all things have taken place. Heaven and earth will pass away, but my words will not pass away. Be on guard so that your hearts are not weighed down with dissipation and drunkenness and the worries of this life, and that day catch you unexpectedly, like a trap. For it will come upon all who live on the face of the whole earth. Be alert at all times, praying that you may have the strength to escape all these things that will take place, and to stand before the Son of Man."

—Luke 21:25–36

Prisoners of Hope

"Be on guard so that your hearts are not weighed down with dissipation and drunkenness and the worries of this life, and that day catch you unexpectedly . . . ." Happy Advent, everyone. Here at the beginning of the church year, we have Jesus talking about what almost sounds like a doomsday scenario. Be on guard, guys, because it's gonna get bad, then it's gonna get worse, then the Son of Man is going to come, and you'll really have to watch out.

That's not what's going on here.

"That day," Jesus said, "be on guard . . . [lest] that day catch you unexpectedly." The day he was referring to was "the day of the son of man," an allusion to Daniel chapter 7. The son of man, or one like a son of man, or a regular dude (depending on how you interpret the words of Daniel), is going to come with the clouds of heaven, and he is going to lead the people of Israel, and from then on, the people of Israel will be honored and praised by all the world, and all nations will look to Israel for peace and justice and the way of God throughout the earth.

This was Daniel 7:13–14, after the first twelve verses of Daniel 7 described four terrible kingdoms of the earth rising up and wreaking havoc on Israel. So, four kingdoms of the earth, followed by a kingdom whose origin is from God, a divinely ordained and ordered kingdom for God's people, Israel.

That hasn't happened yet. If we're looking for historical cognates to the four kingdoms mentioned in Daniel, there are plenty of contenders, like Babylon, Persia, Greece, and Rome, but the point of Daniel's vision is less about particular historical cognates, and more about God's restoration of Israel (and the world) after and even through destruction.

"Be on guard so that your hearts are not weighed down with dissipation and drunkenness and the worries of this life," Jesus said. Remember Daniel's vision. Yes, dark days are coming, and God will be with us, in and through those dark days, and afterwards, we will be restored. "When I am killed," Jesus was saying, "when Rome sacks Israel, and the temple is destroyed, do not become prisoners of despair, weighed down with dissipation and drunkenness and the worries of this life."

Don't become prisoners of despair during the dark times. Whether it's Rome sacking Israel, Hurricane Harvey sacking Houston, the Camp Fire sacking northern California, we have no lack of dark times. We've got distress among the nations, roaring of the seas, fires, floods; we've definitely got fear and foreboding. We've got plenty of reasons to numb ourselves.

That's really what Jesus is talking about, being weighed down by dissipation and drunkenness and the worries of this life. Numbing. Numbing out so the worries of this life seem muted, at least for a little while, and for that little while, we don't have to care as much. Jesus is warning against responding to the worries of this life with dissipation and drunkenness.

Don't be prisoners of despair. Be on guard lest you numb out and spend your life in frivolous amusement, wasteful expenditures, dissolute living . . . basically a lot of excess and pleasure seeking in order to numb out and avoid the darkness and worries of life.

Almost everyone numbs in one way or another to avoid or to get a temporary reprieve from the darkness, despair, and worry of so much going on around us. We all numb out in one way or another, but don't become prisoners of despair, Jesus taught.

Instead, Jesus taught, be prisoners of hope. This idea of prisoners of hope comes from Zechariah 9:12, and I am completely stealing this idea from Rabbi Annie's sermon last month during the Shabbat for Solidarity. Become prisoners of hope.

Jesus knew he was going to die. He knew the Temple would be destroyed and his people would be scattered to the ends of the earth. He was acutely aware of the darkness and hardships around him. He knew things were going to get worse, and yet he remained a prisoner of hope.

Remember Daniel's vision, guys. Remember that one day, God's kingdom will be fully lived out. Remember the brightness of the future which casts out all the darkness of the present. Remember, and be prisoners of hope.

Love deeply. Party with your friends, and enjoy life. That's what Jesus did. Honor and respect yourself and those around you. Be faithful and true to who you are and who you want to be. Serve others when they are in need, and let others serve you when you are in need. Spend lots of time in prayer.

Jesus was constantly reconnecting himself to God through prayer. He got overcome by the darkness of the world, just like we do, and so he spent a huge amount of time reconnecting to the light of God through prayer.

As a people, we're relearning how to reconnect to the light of God through prayer, with ancient practices like centering prayer and meditation.

Praying the hours is becoming cool again. Early in the life of the church, folks were becoming overwhelmed by the fast pace of life and the constant demands of their time and attention by second- and third-century society. So, monastic communities began forming as folks left the cities to devote themselves to quieter lives of prayer. Far from drudgery, lives of service and prayer gave light, life, and joy to those who had been weighed down with dissipation and drunkenness and the worries of this life.

Nowadays, we find a new interest in monasticism in which people don't have to become monks and nuns but can continue to live their regular lives and also join with monastics in lives of service and prayer. More and more folks are choosing to become prisoners of hope. Morning, noon, evening, and night, we Episcopalians pray as prisoners of hope. Even those four times of prayer come from monastic roots, from people no longer wanting to be weighed down by numbing the worries of this life away through dissipation and drunkenness.

Continual prayer and reconnecting to the light of God; serving others in need and allowing others to serve us when we're in need; partying with friends and enjoying life while honoring and respecting ourselves and those around us; and loving deeply—these are the ways Jesus lived as a prisoner of hope, and how Jesus taught us to be prisoners of hope.

Restoration is coming from God. That is our hope. In little ways every day, God is restoring creation in and through us. One day, God will restore all of creation. So do not numb out. Do not be weighed down by dissipation and drunkenness and the worries of this life as prisoners of despair. Instead, love deeply as prisoners of hope.

Free to Grow
3 Advent, Year C
December 12, 2021

> *John said to the crowds that came out to be baptized by him, "You brood of vipers! Who warned you to flee from the wrath to come? Bear fruits worthy of repentance. Do not begin to say to yourselves, 'We have Abraham as our ancestor'; for I tell you, God is able from these stones to raise up children to Abraham. Even now the ax is lying at the root of the trees; every tree therefore that does not bear good fruit is cut down and thrown into the fire." And the crowds asked him, "What then should we do?" In reply he said to them, "Whoever has two coats must share with anyone who has none; and whoever has food must do likewise." Even tax collectors came to be baptized, and they asked him, "Teacher, what should we do?" He said to them, "Collect no more than the amount pre-scribed for you." Soldiers also asked him, "And we, what should we do?" He said to them, "Do not extort money from anyone by threats or false accusation, and be satisfied with your wages."*
>
> *As the people were filled with expectation, and all were ques-tioning in their hearts concerning John, whether he might be the*

Messiah, John answered all of them by saying, "I baptize you with water; but one who is more powerful than I is coming; I am not worthy to untie the thong of his sandals. He will baptize you with the Holy Spirit and fire. His winnowing fork is in his hand, to clear his threshing floor and to gather the wheat into his granary; but the chaff he will burn with unquenchable fire." So, with many other exhortations, he proclaimed the good news to the people.

—Luke 3:7–18

Freed to Grow in Love, Faith, and Hope

Several years ago, after my dad died, Mom gave us his car. It was a newer car than the one I was driving, and better for our family. What to do, then, with the car I had been driving? It had no value to me anymore as a vehicle, but it still had monetary value, so I planned on selling it. A couple of days later, however, I met a gentleman who was in need of a car. He needed a method of transportation to get to and from work so he could keep his job. For him, that car held far more value than the monetary value it held for me. So, rather than sell it, I decided to give it to him.

"Whoever has two coats must share with anyone who has none; and whoever has food must do likewise," John said. Value and usefulness are what's going on in John's teaching. There still may be value in your extra coat, you may still like it, it may even have sentimental value, but if someone doesn't have one, your coat has far more value to that person. For me, the car was no longer useful, and I was glad to give up the monetary value it held for me, because the man's need was greater, and the car's value was greater for him.

Now, John also said, Jesus will "gather the wheat into his granary; but the chaff he will burn with unquenchable fire." The chaff is the outer covering of the wheat, which is necessary while the wheat is growing. It has great value, and if you got rid of it while the wheat was still growing, you'd lose the wheat and the chaff. Once the wheat is grown, however, the chaff loses its purpose and value; it is no longer good for anything but to be thrown out.

While I had only the one car, that car was wheat. It had great value for me so that I could go to work and everywhere else I needed to go. Once Mom gave me the other car, however, my previous car became chaff. It was no longer needed and was no good for me. It needed to be discarded. For the other man, however, my previous car was wheat.

That's part of the good news Luke was talking about when he told the story of John the Baptist and of Jesus burning the chaff with unquenchable fire. One person getting rid of their chaff so that another may have wheat is good news. Viewing our extra stuff as chaff, as things we don't really need, is good news. When we let go of our unneeded stuff, we often find a greater connection to God, a more faithful reliance on God and on others. Trusting in our stuff serves us to some extent, but our stuff doesn't love us. There's no reciprocity, other than that our stuff ends up owning us as much as we own it. A lot of our extra stuff becomes chaff, preventing us from growing.

Remember, the chaff protects the wheat seed when it is growing. Once the wheat is fully grown, however it no longer needs the chaff. Our extra stuff may have served us once, but eventually, it ends up not serving us anymore. The stuff feels useful and protective and probably used to be, but we can't continue to grow if we keep it. So, if we let him, Jesus clears the chaff from the threshing floor of our lives and burns it, helping us grow more in love, faith, and hope.

In addition to our stuff, chaff can also be ways of our lives which may be used to serve us but no longer do. Think of shouting and screaming to get one's way. That works really well for babies and toddlers. They don't have the language to ask for what they want, and they don't have the ability to handle their strong emotions. Now take that same behavior in an adult. The screaming to get one's way worked well as a baby and toddler. As an adult, such a way harms both the person and those around them.

Now, that example is not intended to poke fun at people. I'm guessing many of us have acted that way, screaming and shouting to get our way far beyond the years of infancy. For one thing, we all get too stressed and over-wrought to handle well the things going on in our lives. For another thing, some of us have deeper past hurts and challenges which keep affecting us years and decades after the fact.

The good news which John talked about is that Jesus offers to burn the chaff of those harmful ways in our lives. Jesus offers to heal us, to help us grow in love, faith, and hope.

We continually seek Jesus' help, Jesus' way, Jesus' strength, and for his part, Jesus comes through with his winnowing fork, getting rid of our chaff, getting rid of ways which no longer serve us. Our part, then, is not to fight Jesus, not to hold on to our chaff. Let go the seeming protection of our chaff and allow Jesus to burn our chaff and to heal us.

Letting go of our desires to control that which we can't or shouldn't control.

Chaff which Jesus will burn if we let him.

Letting go of our resentments and desires for vengeance, our rage that things are not right and fair.

Chaff which Jesus will burn if we let him.

Letting go of our refusal to get help when we need it, letting go of our pride and our shame.

Chaff which Jesus will burn if we let him.

I'd love to say this is a one and done kind of deal, but it's more of a daily giving over. A lot of our chaff goes down deep within us. It's not that Jesus doesn't burn it away when we give it to him; it's just that we have far more of it than we realize, and so we give our chaff over to Jesus bit by bit as we recognize it, and I'll be darned if some of it doesn't grow back. So, we keep giving over the chaff of our lives to Jesus and ask him daily to burn it away, to heal us, so that we can be left with the wheat and grow in love, faith, and hope.

Whether the chaff is our extra stuff which no longer serves us or the chaff is ways in our lives which no longer serve us, Jesus' "winnowing fork is in his hand, to clear [the] threshing floor . . . to gather the wheat into his granary . . . [and to] burn [the chaff] with unquenchable fire." That's the good news of Jesus healing us. The good news of Jesus clearing out the things and the ways which no longer serve us but keep us trapped in the past or in our own prison-like shelters which we make for ourselves. We offer those things to Jesus, and Jesus burns them away so that we may be freed to grow as wheat, to grow in love, faith, and hope.

"I love this plan; I'm excited to be a part of it!"[46]
4 Advent, Year B
December 20, 2020

In the sixth month the angel Gabriel was sent by God to a town in Galilee called Nazareth, to a virgin engaged to a man whose name was Joseph, of the house of David. The virgin's name was Mary. And he came to her and said, "Greetings, favored one! The Lord is with you." But she was much perplexed by his words and pondered what sort of greeting this might be. The angel said to her, "Do not be afraid, Mary, for you have found favor with God. And now, you will conceive in your womb and bear a son, and you will name him Jesus. He will be great, and will be called the Son of the Most High, and the Lord God will give to him the throne of his ancestor David. He will reign over the house of Jacob forever, and of his kingdom there will be no end." Mary said to the angel, "How can this be, since I am a virgin?" The angel said to her, "The Holy Spirit will come upon you, and the power of the Most High will overshadow you; therefore the child to be born

---

46 Ivan Reitman, *Ghostbusters* (June 8, 1984: Columbia Pictures).

will be holy; he will be called Son of God. And now, your relative Elizabeth in her old age has also conceived a son; and this is the sixth month for her who was said to be barren. For nothing will be impossible with God." Then Mary said, "Here am I, the servant of the Lord; let it be with me according to your word." Then the angel departed from her.

—Luke 1:26–38

"I love this plan; I'm excited to be a part of it!"
—*Mary, Teenager, Mother of God*

"Do not be afraid," Gabriel said to Mary. He said this in response to Mary's rather nonplussed reaction to his initial salutation, "Greetings, favored one! The Lord is with you," to which Mary seems to have responded about how you might expect a young teenager to respond. "Huh. That's a rather odd way of greeting me, but ok, let's see what this guy has to say."

"Do not be afraid," Gabriel said to Mary, but Mary doesn't seem to have been all that afraid. Maybe she was a particularly brave and trusting young woman. Maybe she was particularly devout in her faith, and she does seem to have been pretty devout. Maybe it was also a good thing that she was a teenager and still invincible like all teenagers are. Had she been in her mid-twenties, it might have been more of a cautious response. "Ok, so what's this gonna mean for me, and how's this all gonna go?"

"Well, kiddo," Gabriel would've responded, "not long from now, your ankles will swell, you're gonna have a hard time sleeping and getting comfortable in general, you're going to be in a lot of pain during the birth, and you'll pee just a little bit every time you cough for the rest of your life. Oh, and most of your family will think you've cheated on Joseph and brought shame upon them, but hey, this child is gonna be hugely important, so your parenting of him has to be . . . not perfect, but at least better than subpar. So, it's ok, don't be afraid."

See, Mary didn't seem to be afraid. All the reasons why following God's plan would be rather troublesome for Mary, those things didn't get in her way. The plan had been pretty much for Joseph and her to get married and have some kids anyway, so Mary seemed rather thrilled at the whole idea. Once Gabriel left, she sang a song about how great it was, not only for her but also for all people, that the Holy Spirit was going to conceive a son in her womb. Her response to Gabriel was not a timid "Let it be with me according to your word" but an enthusiastic "Oh heck, yeah, let it be with me according to your word. This is fantastic."

See, teenager: idealistic, trusting, ready to take on the world and know that it is messed up, beautiful, and worth saving. Mary understood that she was part of God's kingdom on Earth. She was part of God's story of redemption, part of God's story of restoration.

Mary was like Princess Leah in *Star Wars*, ready to take on the whole Empire, stand up to Darth Vader, and lie to his face because she believed in something greater than herself and saw herself as part of a larger story of justice, of ending oppression, of lifting up the lowly, and of casting down the mighty.

[God] has shown the strength of his arm, (Mary sang). He has scattered the proud in their conceit. He has cast down the mighty from their thrones and has lifted up the lowly. He has filled the hungry with good things, and the rich he has sent away empty. He has come to the help of his servant Israel, for he has remembered his promise of mercy, the promise he made to our fathers, to Abraham and his children forever.

All of these things, God has done, Mary sang, in joy and excitement. She knew, and trusted, and loved the God whom she served, and she couldn't wait to be a part of God's story and to see what God had in store for Israel and the world through her and her son. She didn't know exactly what was coming, but she knew redemption was coming. She knew restoration was coming. She knew wrongs were going to be righted. She knew that God's kingdom was coming.

She knew that God's kingdom is a kingdom of love, a kingdom where God's power is used to lift up the lowly, to feed the hungry, and to show mercy. God's kingdom is a kingdom of love in which our power and our wealth are used not to gain more power and wealth for ourselves. In God's kingdom, our power and our wealth, whatever power and wealth we have, are used to lift up the lowly, to feed the hungry, and to show mercy.

Do not be afraid, God tells us, for fear leads to turning away from God's kingdom. Fear keeps us small. Fear keeps us focused on ourselves. Fear tells us that we aren't enough, that we don't have enough, that we can't do the right thing, that we won't be ok. Now, we all have fears, and we all are afraid in various ways. The key is not to let those fears rule our lives.

Mary may well have had some fears of losing her family, of losing her husband, but her teenage brain saw the beauty of God's kingdom, saw the light of God's presence burning throughout creation and said to her fears, "Nah, it'll be ok." So how do we get past our fears and keep that teenage brain gloriously excited about living God's kingdom and saying, "Nah, it'll be ok," to our fears?

One way is to follow the advice of Jedi Master Yoda, to "Train [ourselves] to let go of everything [we] fear to lose."[47] Imagine living without those things that we fear to lose and feeling God's presence with us even in that loss. Jesus had the same advice for a young man who, like Mary, wanted to live God's kingdom, but who also many possessions and was afraid to give them up. Go and sell all that you have, and then come, and follow me (Luke 18:22 [author's paraphrase]), Jesus said, and the man walked away, sad because he didn't want to give up what he had. His stuff, and fear of living without his stuff, kept him from living God's kingdom. He could not let go of that which he feared to lose, so he no longer had the teenage brain to see the beauty of God's kingdom and say to his fears, "Nah, it'll be ok."

In this time of Advent, of preparation for Jesus always coming into the world, we are reminded to train ourselves to let go of everything we fear

---

47   George Lucas, *Star Wars Episode III: Revenge of the Sith* (May 19, 2005: Lucasfilm Ltd.).

to lose. We are reminded of Jesus' teaching to let go of whatever is keeping us small and focused on ourselves. We get to hear again the Angel Gabriel's words, "Do not be afraid."

Do not be afraid of losing what you have in the service of others. Do not be afraid of losing what you have in the service of God's kingdom, for God lifts up the lowly. Train yourself to let go of everything that keeps you from living God's kingdom. Spend time each day in prayer, seeking God's will and God's way. Pray over what you have and what you fear to lose, and pray that all of it may be used for God's kingdom, whether by you or by someone else. Talk and pray with others, your family and friends, seeking together how to follow God's will and way, how to live God's love, redemption, restoration, justice, and mercy.

That is the way of God's kingdom and the way of Mary who knew, and trusted, and loved the God whom she served and couldn't wait to be a part of God's story. She saw the light of God's fire throughout creation, loved God's plan and was excited to be a part of it.

"I love this plan; I'm excited to be a part of it." In addition to being a quote from Bill Murray in *Ghostbusters*, that is the response God is looking for when we catch a glimpse of God's kingdom and our part to play in it. Fear schmear. "How is God calling me to be a part of God's story of love, redemption, restoration, justice, and mercy?" What makes my non-fearful Mary-like teenage brain say, "I love this plan; I'm excited to be a part of it" and "Oh heck yeah, let it be with me according to your word?"

CHAPTER 19

Christmas Sermon

If Ever There Was a Time for Some Almighty Badassery . . .
2 Christmas, Year C
January 2, 2022

In the time of King Herod, after Jesus was born in Bethlehem of Judea, wise men from the East came to Jerusalem, asking, "Where is the child who has been born king of the Jews? For we observed his star at its rising, and have come to pay him homage." When King Herod heard this, he was frightened, and all Jerusalem with him; and calling together all the chief priests and scribes of the people, he inquired of them where the Messiah was to be born. They told him, "In Bethlehem of Judea; for so it has been written by the prophet: 'And you, Bethlehem, in the land of Judah, are by no means least among the rulers of Judah; for from you shall come a ruler who is to shepherd my people Israel.'" Then Herod secretly called for the wise men and learned from them the exact time when the star had appeared. Then he sent them to Bethlehem, saying, "Go and search diligently for the child; and when you have found him, bring me word so that I may also go and pay him homage."

When they had heard the king, they set out; and there, ahead of them, went the star that they had seen at its rising, until it stopped over the place where the child was. When they saw that the star had stopped, they were overwhelmed with joy. On entering the house, they saw the child with Mary his mother; and they knelt down and paid him homage. Then, opening their treasure chests, they offered him gifts of gold, frankincense, and myrrh. And having been warned in a dream not to return to Herod, they left for their own country by another road.

Now after they had left, an angel of the Lord appeared to Joseph in a dream and said, "Get up, take the child and his mother, and flee to Egypt, and remain there until I tell you; for Herod is about to search for the child, to destroy him." Then Joseph got up, took the child and his mother by night, and went to Egypt, and remained there until the death of Herod. This was to fulfill what had been spoken by the Lord through the prophet, "Out of Egypt I have called my son."

When Herod died, an angel of the Lord suddenly appeared in a dream to Joseph in Egypt and said, "Get up, take the child and his mother, and go to the land of Israel, for those who were seeking the child's life are dead." Then Joseph got up, took the child and his mother, and went to the land of Israel. But when he heard that Archelaus was ruling over Judea in place of his father Herod, he was afraid to go there. And after being warned in a dream, he went away to the district of Galilee. There he made his home in a town called Nazareth, so that what had been spoken through the prophets might be fulfilled, "He will be called a Nazorean."

—Matthew 2:1–15, 19–23

If Ever There Was a Time for Some Almighty Badassery . . .

As much as we all know Herod is the bad guy of this story, if a delegation of foreign emissaries came to the president, a couple years into his term, asking to see the other guy who had just been elected president, even though no such election had taken place, it would cause a bit of a stir. People from other nations inexplicably recognizing some new ruler of our country, other than the duly elected president? Where did they hear about this guy? How many others are calling him "President"? Is he a Republican, Democrat, or Libertarian or Green Party? What in the heck is going on?

That's kinda similar to the situation in which King Herod found himself. You can imagine the destabilizing nature a new king being born and foreign nations already recognizing him as king, when he's barely a child, and the current King of Israel has no idea about any of it. What's Rome gonna think? If word of this new king got out, would Rome see Israel as trying to covertly bring about some warlord to start another insurrection and overthrow the Roman Empire?

Herod's consternation makes a good deal of sense, and at the same time, he is aware of a promised, God-anointed Messiah who would come and bring about something like what the prophet Jeremiah spoke of:

> *The Lord has ransomed Jacob, and has redeemed him from hands too strong for him . . . Their life shall become like a watered garden, and they shall never languish again . . . the young women shall rejoice in the dance, and the young men and the old shall be merry. The Lord will turn their mourning into joy, will comfort them, and will give them gladness for sorrow.*
>
> *(Portions of Jeremiah 31:7–14)*

As king, Herod was supposed to be a chief religious leader as well as a civic leader. If he thought the Lord's Messiah had come, it was his kingly duty to help the child grow into the full stature of God's Messiah.

Perhaps Herod was just too much of a pragmatist to do so, as following such a path would certainly have led to a harsh and murderous response from Rome. Perhaps he was just too in love with his own power to want to share it. Perhaps he didn't really believe in God's Messiah in the first place.

Whatever the reason, he felt the wisest course of action was to find the child and kill it as soon as possible. Rather than accept what had come his way, do the right thing, and risk the consequences, he opted for murder.

Of course, he had all the power needed to do so. He didn't like how things were turning out; he had plenty of power to change how things were going, so he chose to do just that. He put a hit out on a toddler, and as we find out in another portion of this story, when he found out his initial attempt to kill Jesus went awry, he had every male child under two years old killed. He had all the power he needed to make things go his way, and he used that power to commit mass murder.

Now, when Herod decided that killing toddlers was a good idea, Mary and Joseph were told that Herod was trying to kill Jesus, and they were told to flee. By this time, they had started something of a life together in Bethlehem. Rather than days or weeks after Jesus' birth, this was likely over a year after that night with the animals and the manger. They were in a house. They'd left home to go to Bethlehem less than two years prior, and now they had to pack what little they could, leave most of what they had behind, and start over again in Egypt.

I can't imagine they were overly happy about this. We don't know what their personal conversations were and any harsh words they might have had privately for the king. We do know that they went. No talk of the injustice of it, no attempt to rally support or start an uprising, no Facebook posts about how terrible the king was. They simply accepted what was, accepted what they were powerless to change, and did what they needed to do.

Herod, in his power, stands in stark contrast to Mary and Joseph. Herod was powerful and abused his power when he would not accept that things were not going his way. Mary and Joseph, powerless, accepted what was, and did all they could to protect their son.

Herod, in his power, also stands in stark contrast to God and God's use of power when God became human.

If ever there was a time for some almighty badassery, it was when God showed up on Earth as a human being. He really could have done anything he wanted. He could have appeared as an adult, walked up to Herod's court, and punched him in the face from 50 feet away. If Herod attacked him with soldiers, he could have turned their swords to feathers, and stuck their feet to the ground so they couldn't move. He could have routed the Roman army with fire from his hands, destroyed them all, and taken Herod's place on the throne of Israel. Any assassination attempt by a distant archer, and the arrows would have been stopped mid-flight by an impenetrable, invisible barrier. Superman wouldn't have had nothing on God, the unstoppable human.

Of course, that's not how God chose to come among us. When God became human, he chose to come among us as a baby, powerless. For his parents, he also chose the powerless: two regular folk who had to flee their city and their country in order to escape the powerful, mad king.

That's how God came to us. As a human, God gave up, or didn't use, the power to destroy nations. Instead, as a human, God used his almighty power to heal the sick, to care for the downtrodden, to feed the hungry. As a human, God used his almighty power to bring connection and love to the lonely and outcast. As a human, God used his almighty power not to force his way upon humanity, but to live in love as best he could, and to invite others to do the same.

That's how God showed us how to be human. As God, Jesus could have railed, and fought, and prevailed against all the terrible things in the world which we cannot change. As a human, however, Jesus chose not to because much of those terrible things in the world are things which we cannot change by our railing and fighting. Jesus showed us instead how to change the world by doing the right thing. Jesus showed us how to change the world by accepting our often powerlessness, rather than forcing our will on others. Jesus showed us how to change the world by trusting in God, regardless of the risks. Jesus showed us how to change the world by healing the sick, caring for the downtrodden, and feeding the hungry. Jesus showed how to change the world by connecting with the lonely and offering love to the outcast. Jesus showed us how to live, how to be human, not as Herod and God, the unstoppable human, but as Mary, Joseph, and their powerless child, Jesus.

CHAPTER 20

Lent Sermons

Living into Our Innate Goodness
2 Lent, Year C
March 13, 2022

> *At that very hour some Pharisees came and said to him, "Get*
> *away from here, for Herod wants to kill you." He said to them,*
> *"Go and tell that fox for me, 'Listen, I am casting out demons*
> *and performing cures today and tomorrow, and on the third day*
> *I finish my work. Yet today, tomorrow, and the next day I must*
> *be on my way, because it is impossible for a prophet to be killed*
> *outside of Jerusalem.' Jerusalem, Jerusalem, the city that kills the*
> *prophets and stones those who are sent to it! How often have I*
> *desired to gather your children together as a hen gathers her brood*
> *under her wings, and you were not willing! See, your house is left to*
> *you. And I tell you, you will not see me until the time comes when*
> *you say, 'Blessed is the one who comes in the name of the Lord.'"*
>
> —Luke 13:31–35

Living into Our Innate Goodness

Jesus was going to do the right thing and follow God's will, regardless of the cost. "Herod's trying to kill you, Jesus; you gotta get out of here!" Nice try, Pharisees, with your fearmongering. We know the Pharisees weren't Jesus' biggest fans, and we know Herod didn't have Jesus arrested in Jerusalem; that was the chief priests and the scribes. So, it seems the Pharisees were just making up a story about Herod trying to arrest Jesus to try to scare him and keep him out of Jerusalem. He threatened their power and authority, so they wanted him gone. Jesus then called their bluff and hinted that he knew he would be killed once he got to Jerusalem and that he was going there anyway.

"Jerusalem, Jerusalem, the city that kills the prophets and stones those who are sent to it!" Years past in Jerusalem, there was idolatry, the leaders of the city turning to false gods to rule the people. They weren't always trying to be sinister. Many were likely trying to lead well, at least at first. They then had power and wealth, and those are hard things to give up. Turning back to God could risk that power and wealth. Even for those who truly wanted to lead well, turning back to God meant risking not only their own position but also the people they served. They were afraid. If they were leading the people, could they really trust the people to God? Could they really turn over the reins?

The more one has to lose, the harder it is to let go. That's why Jerusalem often killed the prophets and stoned those who were sent to it. There was too much to risk, too much fear to turn things over to God, and the prophets' messages rubbed right up against that fear.

Jesus' prophetic voice was constantly calling folks to turn from their fears and to trust God with all their lives and all their hearts. That's not something those in power wanted to hear. Jerusalem, Jerusalem, "How often have I desired to gather your children together as a hen gathers her brood under her wings, and you were not willing!" Well, that's God talking there, and there was too much to risk for the powers that were in the city to allow God to gather the people under her wings.

At some point, that desire to keep control away from God goes from almost passive resistance to open rebellion. That's a strong statement, but when we know we're not living as God wants us to and we still won't turn things over to God, that's kinda like open rebellion.

Now, the desire is not really to rebel against God. Very, very few of us would want to be in rebellion against God. Leaders and those in power seldom want to be in rebellion against God. The desire is simply to keep what we have and to be ok. It is often fear that drives wresting control from God, fear and sometimes mistrust of God. If you don't believe God is good or worthy of being in control, then you're not exactly going to turn the reigns over to God, are you?

Fear and mistrust drive much of what nation-states and political parties do. "We don't feel secure enough, so let's invade another country." "What might happen if *they* get elected and gain power? Let's use dirty tricks and unscrupulous, immoral practices to make sure we stay in power." The powers that be, fearfully wresting control from God to make sure things happen according to the ways they know they should go. Fear and mistrust driving those in power.

Fear and mistrust drive much of what we do as well. Fear of losing what we have. Fear and mistrust of the other. Our bodies are kinda wired for fear, to keep us safe from threats and harm. The trouble is, our brains aren't always great at distinguishing actual threats from non-threats, so our fear response tends to kick in more often than it really needs to. "We've never done things like that before." "Who are these new people? They seem strange." "Will I have enough?" "Can I really trust family, friends, and neighbors if I don't have enough?" "Do I really have enough to help out someone else?"

When we fear and don't have trust, we do all kinds of terrible things. Our bodies are wired for it, but . . .

Here's the not-so-secret truth that Jesus showed us. Our bodies are also wired for trust, love, and letting go. We're wired for faith in God and one another, for trust in God and one another, and for love of God and one another. Jesus showed us that over and over as he continually trusted in God and as he continually lived out of his love for God and others.

"Herod's going to kill you!" the Pharisees said. "You tell that fox I'm going to keep healing people right here for the next two days, then I'll be leaving, and soon I'll be coming to Jerusalem." You may be trying to scare me, Jesus was saying, but I'm going to continue to heal people because I love people and because that's what God wants me to do.

We all have that same capacity for trust in God. We all have that same capacity to love others and to overcome our fears in order to love others in what we do and how we live. We have that capacity because that's how God made us. Trusting in God, loving others, overcoming fear—that's how we were made by God. That's part of God's image in which we were made. We were made so, so good, and that goodness is in us every moment of our lives. That's what Jesus shows us about our humanity, and that the more we draw near to God, let go of fear, and turn our will over to God's will, the more we live into our trust, our love, and our innate goodness.

That's what Jesus desires. That's what God desired when wanting to gather the people of Jerusalem under her wings, to release them of their fear so that they would more fully love and trust one another and live into their innate goodness. That's what God desires for all of us.

Think of the challenges and conflicts in your lives that could be so greatly diminished and even healed by releasing your fears, fully loving and trusting God and others, and living into your innate goodness. Think of all the suffering, the conflict, the wars that wouldn't happen if rulers and those with power would release their fears, fully love and trust God and one another, and live into their innate goodness. Now, we can't control the powers that be, and we're not exactly going to end all war by choosing to let go of fear, to love and trust God and one another, and to live into our innate goodness, but it's a start.

Contra the Pharisees' warning in our heads, Herod's not trying to kill us. The stuff we have, and the power we have, our fears may keep trying to tell us that Herod wants to kill us, the wiring in our brains telling us to be afraid, but Jesus is telling us to call our brains' bluff. Jesus is telling us that our brains aren't just wired for fear. Our brains are also wired for trust, love, and letting go. Jesus is leading us to live not into our fears but to turn from our fears and to live into our innate goodness.

A Serpent to Kill the Lizard Brain
4 Lent, Year B
March 14, 2021

> *From Mount Hor they set out by the way to the Red Sea, to go around the land of Edom; but the people became impatient on the way. The people spoke against God and against Moses, "Why have you brought us up out of Egypt to die in the wilderness? For there is no food and no water, and we detest this miserable food." Then the Lord sent poisonous serpents among the people, and they bit the people, so that many Israelites died. The people came to Moses and said, "We have sinned by speaking against the Lord and against you; pray to the Lord to take away the serpents from us." So, Moses prayed for the people. And the Lord said to Moses, "Make a poisonous serpent, and set it on a pole; and everyone who is bitten shall look at it and live." So, Moses made a serpent of bronze, and put it upon a pole; and whenever a serpent bit someone, that person would look at the serpent of bronze and live.*
>
> *—Numbers 21:4–9*

A Serpent to Kill the Lizard Brain

So, imagine you are in a desert, the wilderness, with a few hundred thousand of your closest family and friends, and you get to spend most of your day not hunting or growing crops, not worried about what you're going to have to eat each day because food from Heaven comes down each morning and settles on the ground like dew. You've worked on some housing and shelter, but otherwise, if you want to spend the day playing the lute or pipe and singing and dancing, you pretty much can because God has taken care of your needs.

Then, you start to cry. "We don't like this food! We're gonna die!" That's what was going on with the people of Israel in our story from Numbers today. "We don't like this food (that you give us every day, God)! We're gonna die!"

I think of children on a long car ride, kinda hungry, pretty bored, rather uncomfortable. They probably don't actually think they are going to die of hunger, boredom, thirst, etc. If they were to think long and hard enough about how they're really doing, they might even admit that really, they're just uncomfortable. Listening to the anguished cries of those moderately hungry, bored, and uncomfortable children, however, it sounds like they are indeed in the last throes of starvation and death.

To be fair, I've heard plenty of adults make similar anguished cries of "This is terrible; we're gonna die," when really, they were just uncomfortable or not overly happy with how things were going.

So how did the people of Israel, and how do we, go from the point of uncomfortable and bored to "We don't like this food! We're going to die!"?

Well, it has to do with the way our brains work. There's the thinking part, the frontal part of our brain, which realizes, "Yeah, no, I guess I'm really not about to die; I just need a snack; I'm good." There's also a lower part of our brain, which I call the lizard brain, which has your basic fight or flight function. Lizard Brain sees a threat or a perceived threat, and it starts getting us a little more anxious, a little more agitated. It doesn't know that the hunger we feel isn't actually life threatening. Lizard Brain just knows "hunger bad!" As we go, if Lizard Brain starts to get really scared, it initiates lockdown, a fight or flight response to the real or perceived threat. The thinking part of our brain is actually shut down, and we begin acting and even making decisions based on this lowest lizard part of our brain which simply says, "There's a threat: Eliminate or Run?"

We see this all the time with road rage, with people screaming at a cashier, with family members shouting at one another. When people say something in the heat of an argument that they instantly regret and don't really mean, or when they're in an argument and start making stupid statements that they later realize they don't even believe, that's when Lizard Brain has taken over.

That's the condition of our brains. We really don't like being uncomfortable, we're not overly fond of anxiety, and we absolutely abhor uncertainty. Our brains want resolutions to problems quickly; our brains want to collate information and get it tucked away in the appropriate place so our world makes sense and we feel safe.

When situations or things register in our brains as uncomfortable or possibly threatening, Lizard Brain starts to raise its little lizard head. For the children uncomfortable in the car on the long drive, the lack of comfort brings Lizard Brain to the fore, the fight or flight response kicks in, and you get the anguished cries of children who have just had a snack and yet are starving to death.

So, we have the situation in Numbers in which the people of Israel were railing against God for bringing them out of Egypt just to die of hunger in the wilderness. They were in the desert, they were nomadic, and they were really tired of the miserable food God kept giving them every day . . . they were dying of hunger because they were tired of the food. Israel was not afraid of dying, even though they claimed they were. Israel was on a long car ride, uncomfortable, anxious, and full of uncertainty about the future—three things which Lizard Brain abhors.

As a response, God sent serpents among the people. That seems a bit much as a response to complaining, and certainly not something I would recommend parents do on the car ride. So, other than God being angry and wanting to hurt the people who had slandered him with lies about his mistreatment of them and them being near the point of death, what might be going on with this serpent attack?

I had this idea. What if the serpents were a little less literally poisoning and killing people and a little more poisoning the people as the serpent did in the garden of Eden? There, the serpent poisoned Adam's and Eve's minds with lies.

With that idea in mind, I checked with my favorite rabbi, and one of the coolest people I know, Annie Belford. She pointed me to a commentary by eleventh-century Rabbi Rashi, who wrote about this passage from Numbers:

> "God said, as it were: Let the serpent which was punished for slanderous statements come and exact punishment from those who utter slander. — Let the serpent to which all kinds of food have one taste (that of earth; cf. Genesis 3:14 and Yoma 75a) come and exact punishment from these ingrates to whom one thing (the manna) had the taste of many different dainties (see Rashi 11:8) (Midrash Tanchuma, Chukat 19)."

Like the serpent in Eden, the people of Israel in the wilderness were telling slanderous lies against God: He was killing them, making them starve to death. In fact, God had cared for them and sheltered them and kept them safe and well fed, but Lizard Brain was taking over in the people and so they made their anguished cry of "We're gonna die."

Then, whether God sent serpents which actually killed them with literal venom, or if the serpents were killing them with more deceit and lies, God had Moses set up a bronze serpent for the people who were bitten to look upon and be healed.

Now, this bronze serpent was not like Medusa in reverse. It wasn't magic, as though if it happened to cross into someone's line of sight, suddenly they were all better. It wasn't an idol or a god to bring healing. The bronze serpent worked as people looked upon it and realized, "That's what I've become. I've become as the father of lies, trusting my own anxiety and Lizard Brain rather that trusting in God, who has freed us and kept us safe."

They would look upon the bronze serpent with true repentance and let Lizard Brain quiet down for a few moments, and the serpent would kill the lizard.

That's a big part of religion and religious practices—to help us silence Lizard Brain and return to trust in God and peace in our hearts. See, when we're fully freaked out, thinking, *We don't like this food; we're going to die,* and Lizard Brain is in control, our thoughts and beliefs aren't usually enough to bring us back to trust and peace because the thinking parts of our brains are shut down when Lizard Brain is in control.

We need more than thoughts and belief when Lizard Brain takes over; we need actions, we need habits, we need a bronze serpent, so to speak, to kill the lizard. Thus, we have habits and practices of prayer and meditation, of scripture reading, of silence and breathing, of serving others, of daily turning our lives and wills over to God, and daily taking stock to see how we did and where we might need to seek correction or reconciliation.

That's the idea of Lent. That's the idea of practicing daily habits of our religion, learning over and over to trust God and then, when Lizard Brain does take over, to use our well-established practices as a bronze serpent to kill the lizard.

So, parents, when your children make slanderous cries of how wicked you are for bringing about their imminent death after a few hours in the car with snacks and water ready at hand, I suggest again not releasing a box of serpents on your kids. Rather, I suggest instilling in them or suggesting to them over time a habit of religious practices to help them return to God with trust and peace so they'll have some bronze serpents with them on the long car rides.

For adults who also have times of Lizard Brain hijack, I recommend the same thing: Develop habits over time of religious practices—prayer, meditation, breathing, walking, reading scripture, serving others, creating, noticing beauty. Develop these habits so that they can serve as bronze serpents to kill the lizard brain when it rears its little lizard head, and then return to God with trust and peace.

Reconciliation for the Good Guys and the Bad Guys
4 Lent, Year C
March 27, 2022

From now on, therefore, we regard no one from a human point of view; even though we once knew Christ from a human point of view, we know him no longer in that way. So, if anyone is in Christ, there is a new creation: everything old has passed away; see, everything has become new! All this is from God, who reconciled us to himself through Christ, and has given us the ministry of reconciliation; that is, in Christ God was reconciling the world to himself, not counting their trespasses against them, and entrusting the message of reconciliation to us. So, we are ambassadors for Christ, since God is making his appeal through us; we entreat you on behalf of Christ, be reconciled to God. For our sake he made him to be sin who knew no sin, so that in him we might become the righteousness of God.

—2 Corinthians 5:16–21

Now all the tax collectors and sinners were coming near to listen to him. And the Pharisees and the scribes were grumbling and saying, "This fellow welcomes sinners and eats with them." So, he told them this parable:

Then Jesus said, "There was a man who had two sons. The younger of them said to his father, 'Father, give me the share of the property that will belong to me.' So he divided his property between them. A few days later the younger son gathered all he had and traveled to a distant country, and there he squandered his property in dissolute living. When he had spent everything, a severe famine took place throughout that country, and he began to be in need. So he went and hired himself out to one of the citizens of that country, who sent him to his fields to feed the pigs. He would gladly have filled himself with the pods that the pigs were eating;

and no one gave him anything. But when he came to himself he said, 'How many of my father's hired hands have bread enough and to spare, but here I am dying of hunger! I will get up and go to my father, and I will say to him, 'Father, I have sinned against heaven and before you; I am no longer worthy to be called your son; treat me like one of your hired hands.' So he set off and went to his father. But while he was still far off, his father saw him and was filled with compassion; he ran and put his arms around him and kissed him. Then the son said to him, 'Father, I have sinned against heaven and before you; I am no longer worthy to be called your son.' But the father said to his slaves, 'Quickly, bring out a robe—the best one—and put it on him; put a ring on his finger and sandals on his feet. And get the fatted calf and kill it, and let us eat and celebrate; for this son of mine was dead and is alive again; he was lost and is found!' And they began to celebrate. Now his elder son was in the field; and when he came and approached the house, he heard music and dancing. He called one of the slaves and asked what was going on. He replied, 'Your brother has come, and your father has killed the fatted calf, because he has got him back safe and sound.' Then he became angry and refused to go in. His father came out and began to plead with him. But he answered his father, 'Listen! For all these years I have been working like a slave for you, and I have never disobeyed your command; yet you have never given me even a young goat so that I might celebrate with my friends. But when this son of yours came back, who has devoured your property with prostitutes, you killed the fatted calf for him!' Then the father said to him, 'Son, you are always with me, and all that is mine is yours. But we had to celebrate and rejoice, because this brother of yours was dead and has come to life; he was lost and has been found.'"

—Luke 15:1–3, 11b–32

Reconciliation for the Good Guys and the Bad Guys

In the parable of the Loving Father which Jesus told (commonly called the parable of the prodigal son), there are two sons who can both easily be identified as the bad guys in the parable.

The first son wants his inheritance. "Yeah, thanks for loving me, Dad. You know, you're going to die one day, so might as well be now. Can I have my inheritance from you? The fact that this will wound you deeply is totally irrelevant to me because honestly, I don't care. Just give me my money."

The second son is hacked off that his father is forgiving and loving. "How could you be so stupid, Dad, to celebrate when this wasteful son of yours comes back? Don't you know this is all about me? Don't you know that your love for your son and your deep grief over his leaving are meaningless to me because of me and my feelings? Did you ever think how rejoicing at his return might rub up against my jealousy and feelings of self-righteousness? How could you be so selfish and stupid, Dad?"

Two sons, both, in their own ways, treating their father with total disregard and contempt. They can both easily be identified as the bad guys of the story.

We love stories with easily identifiable good guys and bad guys. Such stores have a nice, simple order to them, and such stories help us to order our world in a nice, simple way. Easily identifiable good guys and bad guys all around us.

Russia has just invaded Ukraine, so: Russia bad, Ukraine good. For those of us who grew up during the Cold War, this one is easy and familiar. Russia bad is a real easy place to fall back into. Our brains even reward us for it. Our brains like order and neat, simple classification and conclusions. Our brains hate ambiguity. So, when we make simple and easy classifications of good guy and bad guy, our brains reward us with dopamine, the feel-good hormone. Russia bad, Ukraine good—brain happy.

We have easily identifiable "Bad Guys" all around us. Drug dealers, bad guys. Abusers, bad guys. Murderers and rapists, bad guys. Countries who invade other countries to gain more power and intentionally kill inno-cents, bad guys.

Of course, the bad guys change depending on who you are. Rich peo-ple, bad guys. Poor people, bad guys. Police, bad guys. White people, bad guys. Minorities, bad guys. Atheists, Christians, Democrats, Republicans, bad guys. Victims of abuse who were once good guys but end up abusing others because of the abuse they suffered, bad guys. Countries who invade other countries to keep others safe and unintentionally kill innocents, bad guys.

There are bad guys and good guys all around us, and those categories change depending on who we are. For many, even the parable of the prodigal son is not a story of two bad-guy sons and a good-guy dad but a story of one bad-guy son, one good-guy son, and a dad who is kinda being a bad guy to his good-guy son.

Good guys and bad guys fit into easy categories that make our brains happy, so they reward us with dopamine. God, however, doesn't seem to view the world in quite those good guy / bad guy terms. Actions, God sees as bad, sure. People are not as easily blown off by God as simply "the bad guys." The Parable of the Prodigal Son (or the Parable of the Loving Father) shows that God doesn't simply classify people as good guys and bad guys. Rather, God classifies people as beloved children in need of healing and love.

For the sake of those beloved children in need of healing and love, God, who knew no sin, became sin on the cross, so that all might be healed and joined to God through God's incarnation. God shared with us all of our sins as well as all of our healed and whole selves. That's because from God's point of view, we are all God's children in need of healing and love.

"Regard no one from a human point of view," Paul wrote. From a human point of view, there are some good people and a lot of bad people. From God's point of view, there are beloved children in various states of hurt and harm, all of whom need healing and love.

Now, healing and love doesn't mean people aren't held accountable for their actions. Jail for crimes? Yes. Accountability for war crimes? Yes. Working through challenges and making amends for past wrongs? Yes.

Holding grudges and never allowing for restoration? No. Withholding the possibility of returning to someone's good graces or to society's good graces? No. Continuing to declare in-groups and out-groups, good guys and bad guys? No. Holding over the heads of those who have wronged us any past hurts they have caused? No.

It's a hard lesson to accept. Our brains fight us on it because they really want the good guy / bad guy classifications, and our brains are ready with a nice little shot of dopamine every time we make those classifications. From God's point of view, however, that dog just won't hunt. Everyone is a bad guy to someone. Everyone is someone's enemy.

If anyone is in Christ, however, that one is a new creation. As new creations, we don't have to regard others as enemies. In Christ, we have been made new creations so that we no longer regard one another as enemies from a human point of view. God has given us the ministry of reconciliation, not to choose, chasten, and declare the good guys and bad guys, but to be ministers of reconciliation, bringing healing and love. Not counting trespasses against others, as ambassadors for Christ, we seek to bring healing, love, and reconciliation between people and to help people realize their reconciliation with God.

People who are loved, healed, and reconciled tend not to commit murder or rape. People who are loved, healed, and reconciled tend not to commit war crimes. People who are loved, healed, and reconciled tend not to make money off of things that harm others. People who are loved, healed, and reconciled tend to care about others, trust others, and seek to heal others, even and especially those who are viewed as bad guys.

We weren't given the ministry of reconciliation to dole out to the good guys (as we see them) and to withhold that ministry from the bad guys (as we see them). We were made new creations in order to regard one another from God's point of view. We were made new creations to live out God's reconciliation in a world and to a people in desperate need of healing and love. We were given God's reconciliation to view people not as bad guys but as good guys who, like all of us, have hurt others and who, like all of us, need healing and love.

CHAPTER 21

Easter Sermon

Starting from a Place of Reconciling Love
3 Easter, Year C
May 1, 2022

After these things Jesus showed himself again to the disciples by the Sea of Tiberias; and he showed himself in this way. Gathered there together were Simon Peter, Thomas called the Twin, Nathanael of Cana in Galilee, the sons of Zebedee, and two others of his disciples. Simon Peter said to them, "I am going fishing." They said to him, "We will go with you." They went out and got into the boat, but that night they caught nothing. Just after daybreak, Jesus stood on the beach; but the disciples did not know that it was Jesus. Jesus said to them, "Children, you have no fish, have you?" They answered him, "No." He said to them, "Cast the net to the right side of the boat, and you will find some." So they cast it, and now they were not able to haul it in because there were so many fish. That disciple whom Jesus loved said to Peter, "It is the Lord!" When Simon Peter heard that it was the Lord, he put on some clothes, for he was naked, and jumped into the sea. But the other disciples came in the boat, dragging the net full of fish, for they were not far from the land, only about a hundred yards off. When they had gone ashore, they saw a charcoal fire there, with fish on it, and bread. Jesus said to them, "Bring some of the fish that you have just caught." So Simon Peter went aboard and hauled the net ashore, full of large fish, a hundred fifty-three of them; and though there were so many, the net was not torn. Jesus said to them, "Come and have breakfast." Now none of the disciples dared to ask him, "Who are you?" because they knew it was the Lord. Jesus came and took the bread and gave it to them, and did the same with the fish. This was now the third time that Jesus appeared to the disciples after he was raised from the dead.

When they had finished breakfast, Jesus said to Simon Peter, "Simon son of John, do you love me more than these?" He said to him, "Yes, Lord; you know that I love you." Jesus said to him, "Feed my lambs." A second time he said to him, "Simon son of John, do you love me?" He said to him, "Yes, Lord; you know that I love you." Jesus said to him, "Tend my sheep." He said to him the third time, "Simon son of John, do you love me?" Peter felt hurt because he said to him the third time, "Do you love me?" And he said to him, "Lord, you know everything; you know that I love you." Jesus said to him, "Feed my sheep. Very truly, I tell you, when you were younger, you used to fasten your own belt and to go wherever you wished. But when you grow old, you will stretch out your hands, and someone else will fasten a belt around you and take you where you do not wish to go." (He said this to indicate the kind of death by which he would glorify God.) After this he said to him, "Follow me."

—John 21:1–19

Starting from a Place of Reconciling Love

"Feed my sheep," Jesus said to Peter. About a week prior to this, Peter had said to Jesus, "I will lay down my life for you." That was on the night Jesus was arrested. Later that night, sword in hand, Peter began fighting to keep Jesus from being arrested. Peter was being true to his word, but Jesus said, "Put your sword away," basically telling Peter, "If you want to lay down your life for me, that's well and good, but violence isn't the way to do it."

So, after Jesus was arrested, without his sword, Peter denied even knowing Jesus. It seems that Peter would only lay down his life through violent action, and beyond that, he really didn't know how to lay down his life for Jesus.

Then in our story today, Jesus shared a meal with Peter on the beach and gave him three opportunities to make amends for having denied him. "Do you love me?" Jesus asked, further teaching Peter how to love him. No violent action, Peter. No fighting with others to force your way in this world, and certainly no violence against others to force my way in this world. If you love me, Jesus said, then feed my sheep.

That's a bit trickier than violent action. To try to love Jesus through violence is extremely easy. Identify a bad guy, and then in your righteousness, say or do things to harm that bad guy or to turn people against them.

Even without resorting to stabbing people or shooting people, the violence we perpetrate against our supposed bad guys is both commonplace and harmful, even the way we write and talk about others. Think of political discourse nowadays. Think of the things we so easily write against our various bad guys on social media. Think of how, even in our thoughts and conversations, we so easily dismiss or denigrate groups of struggling people. Think of big political issues and all of the violence done even in how we talk about these issues.

Folks on all sides of these issues commit terrible acts of violence in how we talk and think about the people involved, how we talk and think about the supposed bad guys in these issues. That's not the way or will of Jesus. All of the people in these issues are beloved children of God. In trying to effect positive change in these issues, the condition of our hearts matters.

Put away your swords, Jesus said. You can't feed my sheep with swords in hand and hearts of violence.

Instead, have a heart that is open to the other, ready to listen even when you don't love what you're hearing. It's also good to do this over a meal.

What did Jesus do with Peter? He cooked some fish, asked Peter to sit down and have a meal with him, and then he invited Peter to listen, and Jesus listened to Peter as well. Jesus didn't tell Peter how bad or wrong he was to have denied him. That would have been violence against Peter. Jesus didn't want to hurt Peter. He wanted Peter to help serve others and to help care for the needs of others. That didn't start from a place of violence and self-righteous haranguing. Feeding Jesus' sheep started from a place of reconciling love.

Back in March, several of us went to a workshop called "In-Common," which addressed community health and causes of poor community health. It was basically a weekend learning about feeding Jesus' sheep. One key learning was to look at root causes, not just presenting issues. They told a parable of three people walking by a river who saw a bunch of kids in the water, struggling, drowning. One of the people immediately started pulling kids out of the water. The second built rafts to help the kids who were still in the water. The third person continued walking upstream. "Where are you going?" the other two asked. "To find who's throwing kids in the water," the third person said.

All three approaches are needed: crisis care, longer term assistance and training, and looking at root causes for why there is poverty and poor health in the first place.

Think of a school with poor test scores, poor attendance, and terrible behavior in the classrooms. Some might try more money for better teachers. Get more counselors to help with the behavior. Send the really disruptive kids to an alternative school where the problem kids go. Of course, none of the problems get solved by those solutions because they are just looking at the symptoms, not the causes.

Why do the kids have poor test scores, poor attendance, and terrible behavior? Say it's an area with high poverty, food insecurity, and very little medical insurance. With such stress and difficulty as underlying causes, there is little that can be done in the classroom to raise test scores. Free student meals definitely help. Kids can't learn when they're hungry. So, that's kind of like building a life raft. Helping in a sustainable way with hunger, one of the causes of the poor test scores. It helps some, but the root causes are greater than that.

So, community leaders gather with parents, share some food, and ask what challenges they face. They share time of reconciling love as the community leaders listen, finding out that parents are under a lot of stress and that stress affects the kids.

They find that one primary source of stress is lack of access to medical care for their kids. There are a couple of doctors near the community, but any doctor's visit means time off work, which means less money coming in for things like food. Also, most of the parents can't afford medical insurance, or they have the high deductible plans that cover only costs after they've spent $7,000, so they have even less money to spend on food, rent, clothes, things like that.

Through the reconciling love of sharing a meal and listening, they've now identified a root cause for family stress, poor attendance, hunger, and the resultant disruptive behavior.

So, the community leaders work with the community, with organizations in the community, with the school board and principal, and they get a free medical clinic in the school itself. Now parents don't have to take time off work to get their kids to a doctor's visit. They have more money for food. They have less stress at home. Test scores, attendance, and behavior within the school all improve dramatically.

That's a true story. That's people feeding Jesus' sheep. No violence or denigrating any villains within the story. Folks got together. They shared a meal. They listened to one another. They shared reconciling love as they worked together to feed Jesus' sheep.

CHAPTER 22

Sermons for the Season After Pentecost

"You Can't Fight in Here. This Is the War Room."[48]
Proper 5, Year B
June 6, 2021

> *. . . And the crowd came together again, so that Jesus and his disciples could not even eat. When Jesus' family heard it, they went out to restrain him, for people were saying, "He has gone out of his mind." And the scribes who came down from Jerusalem said, "He has Beelzebul, and by the ruler of the demons he casts out demons." And he called them to him, and spoke to them in parables, "How can Satan cast out Satan? If a kingdom is divided against itself, that kingdom cannot stand. And if a house is divided against itself, that house will not be able to stand. And if Satan has risen up against himself and is divided, he cannot stand, but his end has come. But no one can enter a strong man's house and plunder his property without first tying up the strong man; then indeed the house can be plundered.*

---

48   Stanley Kubrick, *Dr. Strangelove or: How I Learned to Stop Worrying and Love the Bomb* (January 29, 1964: Columbia Pictures).

"Truly I tell you, people will be forgiven for their sins and what-ever blasphemies they utter; but whoever blasphemes against the Holy Spirit can never have forgiveness, but is guilty of an eternal sin"— for they had said, "He has an unclean spirit."

Then his mother and his brothers came; and standing outside, they sent to him and called him. A crowd was sitting around him; and they said to him, "Your mother and your brothers and sisters are outside, asking for you." And he replied, "Who are my mother and my brothers?" And looking at those who sat around him, he said, "Here are my mother and my brothers! Whoever does the will of God is my brother and sister and mother."

—Mark 3:20–35

"You Can't Fight in Here. This Is the War Room."

Strange as it may sound, today's Gospel reading made me think of a scene from the movie *Dr. Strangelove*, where the U.S. president, a Russian ambassador, and the top U.S. general are all trying to avert nuclear Armageddon when the general and the Russian ambassador start fighting, and the president shouts at them, "Gentlemen, you can't fight in here! This is the war room!" With similar irony, we hear the scribes saying to Jesus, "Jesus, please, you can't heal people here, we're doing God's work!"

How could they think healing people was bad? How could they think casting out demons was bad?

Well, healing and casting out demons wasn't necessarily bad in and of itself, of course, but what if Jesus was turning people to trust in him, rather than in the religious system? What if, even worse, Jesus was teaching something different about God than they were, and was therefore, of course, teaching something terribly, terribly wrong about God?

That, we understand. Think of a new pastor at a new, growing congregation. It's not a church like the established churches are used to, and even some of those established churches' members are going to that new church. They are on fire, they are serving within the community in ways the established churches haven't been doing for decades, and the established churches are all threatened by this new congregation. They don't like the pastor. He's doing things wrong, the church services are weird, and they feel threatened by them doing really well and doing things differently than what they know to be the right way. "Oh sure, they're doing good work there, but yeah, they pray weird."

We get that. We understand the scribes feeling threatened by Jesus, thinking he was leading the people down a wrong path, in spite of his healing and casting out demons. So, what did they do? They demonized Jesus, saying he was doing demonic work casting out demons. It didn't make much sense then either.

Jesus was fighting a spiritual battle against demons and cosmic powers, against spiritual forces of evil in the heavenly places (I grabbed that from Ephesians). To be fair, it wasn't much of a fight against the demons. Jesus was like One-Punch Man, but still, seeing this, the scribes chose to fight with him about it, about who was right and who was wrong, and Jesus' response was basically "Gentlemen, you can't fight in here. This is the war room."

Jesus was saying, "I'm fighting a war against demons" (which was again pretty easy for him "Get out of there, demon!" "Ok."), and the scribes were fighting with him about that. That was the difficult battle, people working against healing and love because they didn't agree with the person who was doing it or the methods they used.

That is still the difficulty we have today. We understand how crazy it is for the scribes to fight against Jesus when he was casting out demons and healing people. We understand how crazy it is for our church or any church to rally against another church when we see them doing good, healing ministry with the community, even if they pray weird, but what about when that church is ministering with the wrong kinds of people, or letting the wrong kinds of people be ministers? What then?

They're still doing great works within the community, still healing and working with people to transform their lives, but it's just the wrong kind of people doing the ministry? What if it's staunch conservatives doing the ministry? What if it's flaming liberals doing the ministry? What if the ministers are people whose beliefs and ideologies not only go against my beliefs and ideologies but also go against who I am as a person?

I don't have a clear-cut answer on this one; however, I will say this about our beliefs and ideologies. The scribes had beliefs and ideologies which led them to discount some people as unworthy of being a full part of their community, of their world. The scribes were concerned with purity and people being religiously correct enough to be acceptable for God.

Jesus, not so much. Jesus was concerned with people causing actual harm to one another. Are you being clean and pure? Jesus didn't seem to ask that. Are you causing actual harm to someone else? That's what Jesus seemed interested in. Are you excluding people you deem unworthy or impure? Are you keeping for yourself far more than you need while others struggle just to have enough? Are you so certain of your own righteousness that you tear others down, condemning them, rather than choosing to love them and taking the risk of being wrong as you see God working in their lives too? That seems the way of Jesus in his spiritual battles, in his war room.

Yes, there is a war room, even for Jesus, but as Paul wrote in Ephesians 6, " . . . our struggle is not against enemies of blood and flesh, but against the rulers, against the authorities, against the cosmic powers of this present darkness, against the spiritual forces of evil in the heavenly places" (Ephesians 6:10–12). Jesus was certainly against these spiritual forces of darkness, against these spiritual forces of darkness as they manifest in people. We don't read too much, however, of Jesus being against people themselves. He wasn't out there stirring up hatred and division, shouting about the folks people should be against. He warned his disciples privately against the teachings of those rather less than helpful leaders, but his focus was not to turn people against one another.

Jesus' focus was on healing people, bringing people together, showing love, offering grace, living forgiveness. That was Jesus' way. Healing, communion, love, grace, forgiveness, that was Jesus' way, even when fighting spiritual battles for and alongside folks whom others felt were the wrong sorts of folks. Healing, communion, love, grace, forgiveness, that was how Jesus fought spiritual battles in his war room, and strange as it may sound, there's no fighting in the war room. At least there's no fighting in Jesus' war room. There's striving against spiritual forces of darkness, and those battles are fought with healing and communion, with grace, and love, and forgiveness.

Cutting Off Hands . . .
Proper 21, Year B
September 26, 2021

> *John said to Jesus, "Teacher, we saw someone casting out demons in your name, and we tried to stop him, because he was not following us." But Jesus said, "Do not stop him; for no one who does a deed of power in my name will be able soon afterward to speak evil of me. Whoever is not against us is for us. For truly I tell you, whoever gives you a cup of water to drink because you bear the name of Christ will by no means lose the reward.*
>
> *"If any of you put a stumbling block before one of these little ones who believe in me, it would be better for you if a great millstone were hung around your neck and you were thrown into the sea. If your hand causes you to stumble, cut it off; it is better for you to enter life maimed than to have two hands and to go to hell, to the unquenchable fire. And if your foot causes you to stumble, cut it off; it is better for you to enter life lame than to have two feet and to be thrown into hell. And if your eye causes you to stumble, tear it out; it is better for you to enter the kingdom of God with one eye than to have two eyes and to be thrown into hell, where their worm never dies, and the fire is never quenched.*

"For everyone will be salted with fire. Salt is good; but if salt has lost its saltiness, how can you season it? Have salt in yourselves, and be at peace with one another."

—Mark 9:38–50

Cutting Off Hands . . .

Have you ever had a terrible empathy fail? You're overcome with emotion, exhausted, and totally stressed out by all that is going on, and you feel completely not good enough for all that is going on. So, you talk to a friend about it. The friend responds with "Oh, that's ok, it was so much worse for me last year." You end up feeling even worse, like you're still not good enough, but now you're also unimportant.

I've been in a workshop for the last couple days called "Dare to Lead," made by and based on the work of Brené Brown. She is a researcher and the author of *Dare to Lead*, *Daring Greatly*, and other books about shame, how destructive shame is for us, and how empathy is the antidote for shame.

Different from guilt, which says, "I messed up, or did something bad," shame says, "I am messed up, and I am bad." Shame is the feeling of being totally unworthy of love and belonging. Alone. Scared. Not good enough. Not worth people's time. One of the major antidotes for shame is empathy. Empathy helps us feel connected to others. Empathy doesn't dismiss our pain, our fears, or the things we've done. Empathy looks at us as we are, warts and all, and says, "I'm here with you; I get it; you aren't alone; and you are totally worthy of love and belonging."

Sadly, a lot of Christian theology says the opposite. We're sinners, totally unworthy, and destined for torment forever. That's what we deserve . . . unless we believe in Jesus. Then, we're still unworthy, but God loves us anyway.

That's a pretty abusive theology. Shame is at its root. You're terrible, unworthy; you don't belong; you're no good; you should be punished. Shame: being unworthy of love and belonging.

Then, according to these theologies, Jesus comes along and says, believe in me, and God won't punish you forever . . . because God loves you. That's what abusers do to their victims. Tear them down, make them feel worthless, and then say, "I love you, and I alone can make you somewhat decent . . . not worthy of love . . . but I alone will love you even though you are totally unworthy."

That's about control, not empathy or love. It's bad theology which turns God into an abuser, rather than a loving God.

See, the truth of our nature is that we are made beautiful, wonderful, and totally worthy of love and belonging. We're not born with some stain of original sin. We're born. Then, we are hurt over time. We fear. We act out. We hurt others out of our own hurt. God is of course not happy with all of the hurt and harm we do, but God does not see us as terrible and totally unworthy of love. God loves us and hates to see us hurting ourselves and hurting one another.

So, to help heal us, God became human, showing us empathy and love. God, Jesus, knows exactly what it's like to be human. Life is hard; being human is hard. It's beautiful and messy and painful—a glorious train wreck and a glorious symphony all at once. By joining with us in being human, God says, "I'm here with you; I get it; you aren't alone; and you are totally worthy of love and belonging."

So then, believing that theology, that we are worthy of love and belonging, believing that God is not just trying to control us with fear and shame, what is Jesus saying with this dismemberment/mutilation lesson?

Well, obviously, Jesus is not literally telling us to cut off our hands or else he'll punish us forever. I know it sounds that way. "It is better for you to enter life maimed than to have two hands . . . and to be thrown into hell." "If you mess up too much, I'm going to hurt you . . . forever." That's not love.

That's shame, control, fear, and abuse. Remember, Jesus loves us, and we are worthy of God's love and belonging. This dismemberment/mutilation lesson, then, cannot be saying, cut off your hand or I'll punish you forever. The lesson cannot be about shaming us and forcing control over us.

Hear the lesson instead in the light of empathy and love, and you'll see that this lesson is about taking seriously the harm we can cause, showing us just how bad that harm can be, and so encouraging us to take big steps to choose instead a way of healing and restoration.

"Golly, cutting off my hand sounds terrible, and Jesus is saying that the harm I can cause to myself and others with my hand can be even worse than that. I can harm other people in ways that are worse than removing my hand; I can in fact harm people in ways that become like Hell on Earth. I don't want to cause harm like that. I mean, I'm often hurt and angry, but gee whiz, I don't want to bring about Hell on Earth. Maybe I oughta seek another way?"

See, this cast into hell part of Jesus' lesson is not really unknown to us. Planes flown into buildings. Being so angry and feeling so alone that it seems like me against the world. Choosing numbing behaviors so much that people never address the problems in their lives, but just keep growing more isolated and resentful. Politicians wanting to win so badly and being so assured of their righteousness that they denigrate the other side as being evil, bringing about such division and strife that we can't even countenance the thought that there may be some good coming from the other side, that freedom and public health become enemies of each other.

We get being cast into hell. We do it to ourselves all the time. Not casting ourselves into Hell on Earth can take drastic change, drastic giving up of something we hold dear and can't imagine being without. Giving up the need to be right in a religious belief and for others to share in that belief. Letting go of resentments and accepting one's own faults so that it is no longer me against the world. Letting go of numbing so that we actually have to work together on life's challenges. Giving up dehumanizing anger and entrenched wrangling over ideological differences so that we don't make things even worse than our fears of what might happen if the other side won.

Giving up these things can feel like cutting off one's own hand, or foot, or eye. It hurts. Jesus is then holding up that pain next to the pain of the hells that we often make and cast one another into. Jesus is showing empathy and love, saying, "I know the healing work is hard, and I also know, as we all know, how much harder life is without that healing work. Even though it can feel like cutting off your own hand, doing that healing work is so much better than living through Hell on Earth."

God loves us, not in spite of us being unworthy of God's love. God loves us as God's children, and we are totally worthy of God's love and belonging. God also teaches us hard lessons because God knows life can be even harder without them. "I'm here with you; I get it," God says. "You aren't alone; and you are totally worthy of love and belonging."

Casting Down Our sIeDlOvLeSs
Proper 18, Year B
September 5, 2021

From there, Jesus set out and went away to the region of Tyre. He entered a house and did not want anyone to know he was there. Yet he could not escape notice, but a woman whose little daughter had an unclean spirit immediately heard about him, and she came and bowed down at his feet. Now the woman was a Gentile, of Syrophoenician origin. She begged him to cast the demon out of her daughter. He said to her, "Let the children be fed first, for it is not fair to take the children's food and throw it to the dogs." But she answered him, "Sir, even the dogs under the table eat the children's crumbs." Then he said to her, "For saying that, you may go—the demon has left your daughter." So she went home, found the child lying on the bed, and the demon gone.

Then he returned from the region of Tyre, and went by way of Sidon towards the Sea of Galilee, in the region of the Decapolis. They brought to him a deaf man who had an impediment in his speech; and they begged him to lay his hand on him. He took him aside in private, away from the crowd, and put his fingers into his ears, and he spat and touched his tongue. Then looking up to heaven, he sighed and said to him, "Ephphatha," that is, "Be opened." And immediately his ears were opened, his tongue was released, and he spoke plainly. Then Jesus ordered them to tell no one; but the more he ordered them, the more zealously they proclaimed it. They were astounded beyond measure, saying, "He has done everything well; he even makes the deaf to hear and the mute to speak."

—Mark 7:24–37

Casting Down Our sIeDlOvLeSs

There have often been times when I've been in a large group of people and found that I had a great fondness for a good many of the people there, and at the same time, I've found a great antipathy for another large part of the group. I'm referring to times when I've been to a sporting event like an Astros game. Folks wearing the Astros shirts and hats, well they're my people. There was this connection, this bond, this belonging we felt for one another. We didn't know anything at all about one another, but we're wearing the same color T-shirt. We belonged together for that night in the tribe of the Astros.

Now the fans in the Yankees shirts, for example, well we just didn't belong together. I may have had much more in common with them, may have liked them immensely more outside of that stadium and in different T-shirts, but for that night, at the game, we were two different groups who did not belong together. I'm overstating things a bit, of course, but forming exclusive groups is something we humans tend to be pretty good at.

"No girls allowed." "No boys allowed." Little kids making their own, often temporary, exclusive groups. It seems innocent enough—it usually is—and children's "No Boys Allowed" and "No Girls Allowed" clubs also show us how, even early in our lives, we tend toward forming like groups that exclude those who are not alike.

This forming of like groups makes some sense. Sometimes people want to be with folks who are most obviously like them. Sometimes, however, these like groups or exclusive groups can end up hurting those who are excluded. Even kids' "boys only" or "girls only" clubs can unintentionally hurt those who are excluded. Some kids grow up not quite sure where they fit, not sure where they belong: with the girls or with the boys. I think of an old friend, Daniel,—as I knew her years ago—now Stephanie, who had this experience growing up. There was no intention of excluding her, and yet there wasn't really a place for her on the playground when the gym teacher said, "Boys over here, girls over there."

Oftentimes we don't mean to exclude; we're just trying to have a group gathered around a particular similarity. Other times, we very much mean to exclude, to exclude those who are deemed as unworthy, undesirable, or not belonging.

"Whites only." "No Jews." "No Irish." "Women need not apply." There are countless ways our society and all societies have excluded others, and the Church, much as it tries to love, has often been a willing part of such exclusion.

In the past, our churches have been intentionally racially segregated. We have kept women out of ministry, even though Jesus and the early Church did not. We've allowed members of the LGBTQIA+ community to be a part of the Church, so long as they were quiet about and hid who they were. That's just a partial list of how the institution itself has excluded groups from the church. Even more are the ways individuals have removed people they felt were undesirable. The disapproving look given, the audible whispers of disdain, the snubbing of some, and the outright statement "you would be happier somewhere else" to others.

Excluding others in the church has a long history, probably as long as the church has been around. Even the earliest members of the church were human and full of the same challenges that we all have, wanting to feel comfortable, wanting to belong, and sometimes excluding others to make sure we felt comfortable in our own belonging.

Even in Jesus' day, before he had established his church, Jesus was a part of this human tendency toward exclusion. When a woman who was a Gentile begged Jesus to cast a demon out of her daughter, he initially refused. He called her a dog. He saw her as unworthy, as undesirable, as not belonging. Jesus was acting as he had been taught. We don't associate with those gentile dogs.

Then, the woman didn't fight Jesus or refute his claim of her beastliness. "Sir, even the dogs under the table eat the children's crumbs," she said. Supporting Jesus' claim, she revealed it for what it was: cruelty and exclusion. It seems that she brought Jesus up short. It seems that his eyes were opened in that moment, that what he had been taught about Gentiles as less-than-human dogs wasn't really the case. Here was not an unworthy dog but a woman and a child. These also were beloved children of God, and Jesus healed the daughter immediately.

Jesus, who was God but also fully human with human limitations and frailties, had been taught one thing about humanity, that there were undesirable less-than-humans, and then when he saw one of these undesirable less-thans up close, he realized that he had been given a false teaching. This woman, and by extension these Gentiles, were not less than humans, but full humans, beloved of God, who were deserving of love and belonging.

Now, you could say when we exclude others that we're only human, also following what we've been taught. That's true enough. Even so, when we exclude others from the church, we don't do so by acting as humans. When we exclude others from the church, we become idolaters, acting as though we were God. It's God's church, not ours, so when we start to proclaim who can be a part of God's church and who cannot, we are moving God out of our way so that we can make God's church what we want it to be. Putting ourselves in God's place, we end up becoming our own idols, ultimately worshipping ourselves, rather than God.

Who is in, and who is out? Who is worthy, and who is unworthy? By the teaching of various days, the out and unworthy were Black people, women, homosexual people, children who made noise or moved, folks without enough money, or folks with the wrong clothes. All of these people have been excluded from the church at various times and places, following accepted norms of the majority at the time, only to have those norms cast out, those idols thrown down, and the people seen no longer as dogs, but as beloved children of God.

What norms, against what people, do we still hold, putting them down as dogs and raising ourselves as idols in God's place? Who would make any of us personally uncomfortable sitting next to us, or preaching to us, or celebrating at this table? Realizing who those people are, remember that they are not dogs, but God's beloved children, and we are not God to exclude them or anyone from God's church.

No longer in charge as gatekeeper, we simply get to enjoy the rich diversity of who God's children are. Astros and Yankees fans. Rich and poor. LGBTQIA+. Cisgender. Heterosexual. Any and all races and skin colors. American. Immigrant. Children. Adults. Felons. Men and women and all those in between. There is such a rich and beautiful diversity of God's children, and God's intention for God's church and God's kingdom is for us to enjoy all of each other. We are one another's family, God's family. No one of us welcomes another as to our church. Rather, we meet one another together, for we all belong here, in God's church as God's family.

The Cloak of Forgiveness, Healing, and Love
Proper 19, Year A
September 13, 2020

> *Then Peter came and said to Jesus, "Lord, if another member of*
> *the church sins against me, how often should I forgive? As many*

as seven times?" Jesus said to him, "Not seven times, but, I tell you, seventy-seven times. For this reason the kingdom of heaven may be compared to a king who wished to settle accounts with his slaves. When he began the reckoning, one who owed him ten thousand talents was brought to him; and, as he could not pay, his lord ordered him to be sold, together with his wife and children and all his possessions, and payment to be made. So the slave fell on his knees before him, saying, 'Have patience with me, and I will pay you everything.' And out of pity for him, the lord of that slave released him and forgave him the debt. But that same slave, as he went out, came upon one of his fellow slaves who owed him a hundred denarii; and seizing him by the throat, he said, 'Pay what you owe.' Then his fellow slave fell down and pleaded with him, 'Have patience with me, and I will pay you.' But he refused; then he went and threw him into prison until he would pay the debt. When his fellow slaves saw what had happened, they were greatly distressed, and they went and reported to their lord all that had taken place. Then his lord summoned him and said to him, 'You wicked slave! I forgave you all that debt because you pleaded with me. Should you not have had mercy on your fellow slave, as I had mercy on you?' And in anger his lord handed him over to be tortured until he would pay his entire debt. So my heavenly Father will also do to every one of you, if you do not forgive your brother or sister from your heart."

—Matthew 18:21–35

The Cloak of Forgiveness, Healing, and Love

So, how many times do we have to forgive? Not just seven times, but seventy times seven . . .times. Now, seven times seventy is 490. Four hundred and ninety forgivenesses would be kinda hard for me to keep track of, so I did some math, using my prayer bracelet. It has fourteen knots, so if I pray to forgive a person on each knot, every day, then I'll reach that 490 number in thirty-five days. So, with this prayer bracelet, I need to pray to forgive someone fourteen times a day for one month and an additional four days or five days, depending on the month.

Ok, I don't think that's quite what Jesus had in mind, although praying to forgive someone fourteen times a day for thirty-five days just might go a long way to help me actually forgive someone and release that burden. We'll get back to that idea, but first I want to take a look at this seventy times seven number that Jesus gives.

The number of times Jesus says we should forgive someone is not arbitrary. The number comes from Genesis chapter 4. Cain killed his brother Abel and then was told that if anyone killed him, he would be avenged sevenfold. See, Cain was afraid that the whole world would be against him for killing his brother, so being avenged sevenfold was a form of protection. If you are killed, you'll be avenged sevenfold. Ok, so murder bad, and lots of vengeance is brought into the world. Then, Cain's great-great-great grandson, Lamech, killed a man, and he was presumably afraid that someone might seek retaliation against him. So, he said, "If Cain is avenged sevenfold, truly Lamech seventy-sevenfold." (Genesis 4:24). That's a lot of vengeance.

So, when Jesus told Peter that he was to forgive as many as seventy-sevenfold times, Jesus was saying, as much vengeance as there is in the world, that is how much you are to forgive.

A total reversal of vengeance upon vengeance. A total reversal of keeping a record of wrongs and demanding punishment or repayment of the debt of those wrongs. A letting-go of vengeance and restitution and seeking instead healing and restoration.

Love is the idea that Jesus gives, not keeping a record of wrongs. Paul tells us in 1 Corinthians 13:5 that love keeps no record of wrongs. Now, in the New Revised Standard Version, it reads love is not resentful. That's a nice summation of "keeps no record of wrongs." Resentment is just that, keeping a record of wrongs.

Resentment says, "I will not let this go; I will not forgive the wrong done to me until it has been avenged seventy-sevenfold." Then, after waiting for a seventy-sevenfold vengeance, our hearts have been turned dark, and we find we are no longer able to forgive. All we can really do at that point is to continue in anger and resentment, the burden having grown more than we can bear, but the burden also having wrapped itself around us like a cloak so tight that we cannot escape its grasp.

Instead of vengeance seventy-sevenfold, Jesus tells us to forgive seventy-sevenfold. As much vengeance as there is in the world, that is how much we are to forgive. In doing so, we unburden ourselves. The cloak of anger and resentment loosens its grip, until we can eventually let that heavy cloak fall to the ground and be clothed instead with the cloak of light, the cloak of forgiveness, healing, and love.

Forgiving others is not about what is owed or what is deserved. Forgiving others is about unburdening ourselves and unburdening them.

I should note that unburdening is not the same as continuing to go back for abuse. "I keep going back and they keep on hurting me." Stop going back. Forgiveness does not mean keep going back. Forgiveness is release, letting go of the debt, erasing the record of wrongs. Forgiveness is letting go of the hurt, knowing it can't be fully restored, and out of love (for self and for the other), releasing the debt, erasing the record of wrongs. You can also stop lending to that person so to speak. With forgiveness, you may need to say, "I can't be around you anymore" or "here are the boundaries I need to be able to be around you." That's ok. I doubt the king in Jesus' story continued to lend to the servant from whom he had forgiven all that debt.

Forgiveness is letting go of the hurt and the desires for vengeance. Remember that love is the idea, love of self and love of the other, and love as forgiveness releases us and each other from the dark, heavy cloak of vengeance. Then love lets us be clothed instead with the cloak of light, the cloak of forgiveness, healing, and love.

Love keeps no record of wrongs, but our brains do, don't they? Our brains keep a record of wrongs; our emotions keep a record of wrongs. They keep these records in our bodies, in our neural pathways, in our senses of sight, touch, smell, hearing, and sound. The record of wrongs is written all over, in, and through our bodies, and so it takes work to erase that record. It takes work to unburden ourselves and to truly forgive.

Now, back to the idea of forgiving someone 490 times, back to the idea of using a prayer bracelet to pray forgiveness over someone 14 times a day for thirty-five days. Doing so would go a long way to help actually forgive someone and release the burden of anger and resentment. As we pray to forgive someone over and over, we start to rewire those neural pathways so that they are no longer focused on vengeance and resentment. They become focused instead on love.

As we pray to forgive someone over and over, we begin to see that person as a broken and sick individual who needs love and healing just as we do. So, forgiving someone 490 times, or 14 times a day for thirty-five days, is probably a good start toward actually being able to forgive that person. We pray over and over to forgive the person who has wronged us, and then we pray, "Lord Jesus Christ, Son of God, have mercy on me." We pray this day after day, month after month, year after year, until our bodies no longer hold the records of wrongs done to us, for love keeps no record of wrongs.

How often are we to forgive? We are to forgive seventy-sevenfold. As much vengeance as there is in the world, that is how much we are to forgive. We work daily at forgiveness, over and over again, and as we work at forgiveness, the grip of the cloak of resentment begins to loosen and eventually falls off, and then, unburdened, we can be clothed instead with the cloak of light, the cloak of forgiveness, healing, and love.

BIBLIOGRAPHY

Alcoholics Anonymous. 4th ed. (New York, NY: Alcoholics Anonymous World Services, 2001), 89. https://www.aa.org/the-big-book

Brené Brown, 2022. https://brenebrown.com/.

Brené Brown. *Daring Greatly.*

Brené Brown. *Rising Strong.*

Browning, Elizabeth Barrett. *Aurora Leigh*, accessed May 16, 2022, *A Celebration of Women Writers*, 2022, https://digital.library.upenn.edu/women/barrett/aurora/aurora.html.

Calvin, John. "The Institutes of Christian Religion Book Three, chapter 15.3", accessed May 17, 2022, *Bible Study Tools, 2022*, https://www.biblestudytools.com/history/calvin-institutes-christianity/book3/chapter-15.html.

de Beauvoir, Simone. *Ethics of Ambiguity.* Accessed May 17, 2022, *Reddit, 2014*, https://www.reddit.com/r/philosophy/comments/23s1tv/how_well_does_simone_de_beauvoirs_ethics_of/.

Donovan, Vincent. *Christianity Rediscovered.* New York: Orbis Books, 1982.

Dr. Strangelove or: How I Learned to Stop Worrying and Love the Bomb, directed by Stanley Kubrick (January 29, 1964: Columbia Pictures), https://www.amazon.com/dp/B000P407K4

Episcopal Church. The Book of Common Prayer and Administration of the Sacraments and Other Rites and Ceremonies of the Church: Together with the Psalter or Psalms of David According to the Use of the Episcopal Church. New York: Seabury Press, 1979.

Firefly. 2002. Season 1, Episode 4, "Jaynestown." Directed by Marita Grabiak. Aired October 18, 2002 on Fox.

Ghostbusters, directed by Ivan Reitman (June 8, 1984: Columbia Pictures), https://www.amazon.com/Ghostbusters-Bill-Murray/dp/B000PEX1IE

Grieb, Kathy. The Story of Romans: A Narrative Defense of God's Righteousness. Louisville, Kentucky: Westminster John Knox Press, 2002.

Grimm, Jacob., Grimm, Wilhelm. Hansel & Gretel.

Hanh, Thich Nhat. Living Buddha, Living Christ. New York: Penguin Group, 2007.

Herzer, Linda Tatro. The Bible and the Transgender Experience: How Scripture Supports Gender Variance. Cleveland: Pilgrim Press, 2016.

Jessica Jones. 2018. Season 2, Episode 1, "AKA Start at the Beginning." Directed by Anna Foerster. Aired March 8, 2018 on Netflix.

Juliana of Norwich. Revelations of Divine Love. Accessed May 17, 2022, The Holy See, https://www.vatican.va/spirit/documents/ spirit_20010807_giuliana-norwich_en.html.

Kulp, Joshua. English Explanation of Pirkei Avot. Accessed September 8, 2022, Sefaria. https://www.sefaria.org/English_Explanation_of_Pirkei_Avo t.5.22.1?lang=bi&with=all&lang2=en

New Revised Standard Version Bible, copyright © 1989 National Council of the Churches of Christ in the United States of America. Used by permission. All rights reserved worldwide.

Niebuhr, Reinhold. The Serenity Prayer. 1933.

Price, John. *Revealing Heaven: The Christian Case for Near-Death Experiences.* New York: HarperCollins, 2013.

Rogue One: A Star Wars Story, directed by Gareth Edwards (December 16, 2016; Lucasfilm Ltd.), https://www.amazon.com/Rogue-One-Story-Theatrical-Version/dp/B01MQTROL1

Soughers, Tara. *Beyond a Binary God.* New York: Church Publishing, 2018.

Star Wars Episode III: Revenge of the Sith, directed by George Lucas (May 19, 2005: Lucasfilm Ltd.), https://www.amazon.com/Star-Wars-Revenge-Theatrical-Version/dp/B00VF0MBHY

Star Wars Episode V: The Empire Strikes Back, directed by Irvin Kershner (May 21, 1980; Lucasfilm Ltd.), https://www.amazon.com/Star-Wars-Empire-Strikes-Back/dp/B00VF19CBQ

Steindl-Rast, David. *Gratefulness, the Heart of Prayer: An Approach to Life in Fullness.* Mahwah, New Jersey: Paulist Press, 1984.

Terri Hendrix, "Bury the Devil," track 2 on *The Slaughterhouse Sessions Project 5.2,* Terri Hendrix Music, 2016, CD

The Princess Bride, directed by Rob Reiner (September 25, 1987; 20th Century Fox), https://www.amazon.com/Princess-Bride-Cary-Elwes/dp/B000VEPL2M

Tao Te Ching, translation by Gia-Fu Feng, Accessed September 8, 2022, Tao Te Ching - Lao Tzu - A Comparative Study, https://www.wussu.com/laotzu/laotzu79.html

Tao Te Ching, translation by J.H. McDonald, Accessed September 8, 2022, Microsoft Word – Tao Te Ching – trans. by J.H. McDonald, https://www.unl.edu/prodmgr/NRT/Tao%20Te%20Ching%20-%20trans.%20by%20J.H..%20McDonald.pdf.

Tao Te Ching, translation by Stephen Mitchel, Accessed September 8, 2022, Terebess Asia Online (TAO). https://terebess.hu/english/tao/mitchell. html#Kap15

White, L. Michael. *L. Michael White.* Accessed May 17, 2022. https://www. lmichaelwhite.com/.

White, L. Michael. *The "H" Word: What the Bible Says About Homosexuality.* YouTube. May 29, 2012. Accessed May 17, 2022. https://youtu.be/ jraG8Xhounk